KT-199-285

# KARAJAN

Paul Robinson

Discography by Bruce Surtees

Macdonald and Jane's · London

KENT COUNTY LIBRARY EG5509
789.5/KAR

**The Art of the Conductor**

**KARAJAN** *to be followed by*

STOKOWSKI
BOEHM
SOLTI

ISBN 0 354 04031 6

Copyright © 1975 by Lester and Orpen Limited
All rights reserved

First published in Great Britain in 1976 by
Macdonald and Jane's Publishers Ltd
Paulton House
8 Shepherdess Walk
London N.1

WITHDRAWN

Printed in Great Britain by
REDWOOD BURN LIMITED
Trowbridge & Esher

Photographs appear after page 76.

# Preface

I have often wondered why there were so few reliable books on important conductors, especially in English. There have been many Toscanini books, of course, but even these were more often obscure than illuminating. Too many of them were gossipy in the extreme and more interested in quirks of personality than in the musician.

This book, and the others to follow in the series, attempt to make available to both the general and the specialist reader the facts about important conductors, past and present. They also seek to provide a critical evaluation of each conductor's work in terms of technique, repertoire, strengths, and weaknesses. Finally, in every book in the series there is a complete discography. Discographies are regularly compiled in record magazines, but they should be available in a more permanent form.

The series begins with Herbert von Karajan because he is by far the most important living conductor in terms of the major positions he has held, the number of recordings he has made, and the publicity surrounding his name. He is also, in my opinion, the finest conductor of his time with respect to both orchestral control and interpretative insight. As for sceptical readers I hope they will give me the benefit of the doubt until they have read through the book.

Karajan's life and career are discussed in Chapters 1-7,

while a critical discussion of his work is given in Chapter 8. Those familiar with the details of his life may wish to skip directly to Chapter 8, while others less concerned with the somewhat technical matters dealt with in that chapter can confine themselves to the other chapters. But it is Chapter 8 in particular which hopefully will stimulate ongoing discussion of this sort about conductors and conducting. Philosophers of music have not as yet had much to do with this subject, but it is about time they did. Certainly there are all sorts of tough questions which ought to be discussed. But they tend to be obscured by the inevitable anecdotes and superficial criticism that surround such glamorous public figures.

I had been thinking about writing something on Karajan for a long time but the stimulus to really do so came from John Twomey, former manager of radio station CJRT-FM in Toronto. The preparation of scripts for a 30-week series of programs on Karajan beginning in 1972 enabled me to assemble all the material required for this book. Concerning the subject matter itself, I am grateful for the help given me by many critics, musicians, and interested observers, among whom the following should be mentioned (although they are in no way responsible for the use I have made of their comments): Martin Mayer, Paul Henry Lang, Martin Bookspan, Peter Csobadi, Erwin Feher, Lili Chookasian, Helga Dernesch, Karl Ridderbusch, Rainer Zepperitz, James Galway, Michel Debost, Alexis Weissenberg, Michel Glotz, Robert Charles Marsh, Ward Botsford, Franz Kraemer, Ernst Hauesserman.

Part of Chapter 7 was published in the November 1973 issue of *Sound* magazine.

2

# Introduction

When the players of the Berlin Philharmonic had finished tuning, a breathless silence fell over the audience; the orchestra, too, seemed tense and expectant. Then the conductor appeared, walking slowly from the back of the orchestra to the podium. The whole orchestra rose as one in a silent gesture of respect. The audience broke into sustained applause of shattering intensity. By the time the conductor mounted the podium to take a bow, shouts and whistles had broken out. Before any inkling of his musicianship could be discerned, this conductor had excited his audience the way only a great actor can before he utters a line.

But then, before the applause could die, he was into the music. With a downbeat of breathtaking authority and grace the *Eroica* Symphony was underway. And throughout the long symphony the conductor stood as if rooted to the spot, with only his arms in motion. He conducted as if in a trance, his eyes closed, his handsome, rough-hewn features taut with nervous energy. With only the slightest gesture the orchestra would surge with a fortissimo that made one's hair stand on end. Without any knee-bends or fingers to lips, the conductor reduced the sound of the orchestra to the merest whisper. So rarely did this man give any of the usual cues that he seemed to be conducting his own invisible orchestra. Yet there was no doubt that this extraordinary

3

realization of the *Eroica* Symphony was his creation. The performance was prepared to perfection and executed with the utmost concentration and commitment. Rarely had one ever seen professional musicians play with such involvement. In some mysterious way this man was able to galvanize orchestra and audience alike and bring them to give their very best. And throughout the fifty-minute performance of the symphony nothing existed for either conductor or players except the experience of Beethoven's compelling vision.

The conductor was Herbert von Karajan.

Karajan has become a living legend: a master conductor who has built the Berlin Philharmonic into what is generally regarded as the world's finest orchestra. Karajan is also stage and lighting director of nearly all his own opera productions at Salzburg, the Met, and elsewhere. He has been one of the first to explore the field of opera films and concerts for television, using imaginative new visual techniques. He is also the originator of the Karajan Foundations, which hold periodic competitions for young conductors and undertake research in the field of music. Moreover, he has even subjected himself to experiments to test the effects of drugs on musical perception.

As a personality, Karajan is both a glamorous and charismatic figure. The public knows him as a whirlwind of energy, bounding from ski slope to opera house, from sports car to concert hall, from racing yacht to recording studio. He is married to a former French fashion model and hobnobs with the jet-set in St. Moritz and St. Tropez.

As a musician and a man Karajan is one of the most discussed and admired figures in Europe today. Yet, for all the gossip and vituperation about him, Karajan remains something of an enigma. To what extent was he committed to the Hitler regime during his phenomenal rise to fame in pre-war Germany? How can we reconcile the glamorous public image of the man with his well-known aversion to

4

social gatherings of any kind and his rigorous personal discipline that includes two hours of yoga a day? And is it fair to say with Paul Henry Lang of *Musical Quarterly* that Karajan simply "tried to do too much and spread himself too thin?" Is it fair to characterize his performances as "narcissistic" and "overrefined"? as Martin Bookspan has done in *Stereo Review*? Are such judgements to be believed when Karajan turns down virtually all offers of guest conducting and performs only under optimum conditions in Berlin and Salzburg; or when one witnesses the Dionysian excitement he is capable of whipping up in orchestras and audiences alike?

This book is an attempt to unearth all of the relevant facts about Karajan, from his early years as a student to his present eminence, and to try to sort out, on the basis of these facts, what is most remarkable about the man and the artist. Above all, I have tried to give the English reader and music lover access to the truth about Karajan and, therefore, a means by which he can make up his own mind about the man and his music-making. Whether the reader agrees with my assessment of Karajan or not, I hope I will at least have provided him a basis from which he can form his own judgement.

# 1
# The Early Years – 1908–1945

The Karajan story begins, appropriately enough, in Salzburg, the city of Mozart's birth, and the place in which, next to Berlin, Karajan performs most often. Herbert von Karajan was born in Salzburg April 5, 1908.

Though an Austrian by birth, the Karajan family was actually Greek, the original surname being Karajanis or "Black John". The family had migrated from Greece to Chemnitz, Germany, and from there to Austria about four generations before Herbert. The aristocratic prefix "von" was the result of *two* baronetcies that were bestowed on the family: the first in Germany by the Hohenzollerns, for success in the textile business; the second in Austria by the Hapsburgs, for the Karajan family's contribution to public health.

At the time of Karajan's birth Salzburg was far from being the musical centre and tourist mecca it is today. It did not even have the Salzburg Festival to attract attention until 1920. In some ways the Salzburg of 1908 was much as Mozart had left it – a town of quiet Austrian charm on the banks of the Salzach river, dominated by the Hohenzollern Castle on a high hill in its midst.

Its importance, however, stemmed from the place it occupied in musical history. Like so many Austrian or German towns of any size, it had a bustling theatre and opera house. In addition, it was the birthplace of Mozart after whom its music school, the Mozarteum, was named.

Though the Salzburg of 1908 was by no means a musical centre of international repute, it did have a substantial cultural life in which the Karajan family participated. Karajan's father, a doctor at the Salzburg *Krankenhaus*, also found time to play second clarinet in the Mozarteum Orchestra. Karajan and his older brother Wolfgang were exposed to music from an early age and both showed a prodigious talent for it. Wolfgang von Karajan is well-known in Europe today as an organ maker and leader of an organ ensemble.

Herbert gave public performances of Mozart on the piano before he was ten years old and played in public so frequently thereafter that it was clear he was intent on a career as a concert pianist. Throughout his early youth in Salzburg, Karajan studied at the Mozarteum. The late Bernhard Paumgartner, director of the Mozarteum, recognized his special talent before almost anyone else, and took a fatherly interest in Karajan. Karajan could often be seen tearing around the countryside on Paumgartner's war-service motorcycle, and it was Paumgartner who introduced Karajan to painting and sculpture in the great Italian museums.

Late in his teens Karajan left Salzburg for Vienna and began studies at the University of Vienna and the Academy of Music. At the Academy he studied conducting for the first time in his life with Alexander Wunderer, director of a number of musical organizations and a very popular figure in Vienna, both as a man and an artist, but, according to Karajan, leaving much to be desired as a teacher.

What a young conductor desires more than anything else is to conduct an orchestra. Unfortunately, in Karajan's case, as in so many others, there was no orchestra available for the class: students simply beat time while others played the piano. The only valuable feature of the classes was that they were often devoted to the study of scores to be performed at the Vienna State Opera. Students read through the operas singing all the parts, and then went to the opera house, trudging up to their student seats in the fourth gallery to see and hear the real thing.

Karajan does not recall learning much about conducting from the class — that came later in the form of on-the-job training. But he did learn a great deal of opera repertoire. What better environment for the development of a young musician, in any case, than the Vienna *Staatsoper* in its golden age? In addition to all the operas of Richard Strauss and Puccini, Karajan was able to hear, in the years 1924 to 1929, modern works such as Hindemith's *Cardillac*, Krenek's *Jonny Spielt Auf*, and Stravinsky's *Oedipus Rex*, and watch the leading conductors of the day, including Furtwaengler, Clemens Krauss, Richard Strauss, and, later, Toscanini and Bruno Walter.

Though Karajan during his student years immersed himself in the study of repertoire and attended musical events in Vienna, he had not as yet had the opportunity of conducting an orchestra.

At the age of twenty he got his chance. At a concert conducted by Wunderer's students with the Academy Orchestra in Vienna in December of 1928, Karajan made his conducting debut with Rossini's *William Tell* Overture.

This brief exposure, however, hardly satisfied his desire to conduct. And since the Vienna concert failed to produce offers of further employment, Karajan saw that he would have to create his own opportunities.

Since he was well-known as a pianist in his native Salzburg, Karajan had no difficulty in hiring an orchestra and selling tickets for a concert of his own. On January 23, 1929, he appeared for the first time in public conducting a professional orchestra, in a program designed to show off his talents to the full, which included the Strauss tone poem *Don Juan* and the Tchaikovsky Fifth Symphony. The concert was a great success and yielded precisely what Karajan had hoped for: his first appointment to a conducting post.

In the audience that night was the Intendant of the Ulm State Theatre. When he offered Karajan a job that involved mostly opera conducting, Karajan replied that, to be quite truthful, he had never conducted any opera and that he would have to study it. The Intendant was absolutely non-plussed. "Fine," he said, "come and study it," and Karajan was hired for the princely sum of twenty dollars a month to provide opera for the people of the little German town of Ulm, and equally important, to learn his craft as a con-ductor. Less than two months after the Salzburg concert he appeared for the first time in Ulm conducting Mozart's *Marriage of Figaro.*

Ulm was not Vienna or Berlin, nor even Cologne or Dresden. Karajan was in charge of an orchestra of seventeen players for operetta, and twenty-six for opera. The stage itself was no bigger than a large room, and the modest resources of the theatre required him to involve himself in every aspect of opera production including raising and lowering the curtain on occasion. The orchestra rehearsed in a local restaurant and the instruments were transported to the theatre in a wheelbarrow.

In spite of the totally inadequate conditions at Ulm, Karajan had a chance to learn the nuts and bolts of opera production and conducting, and has repeatedly cited such experience as being vital to a young conductor. Karajan is also grateful that he had the opportunity to learn away from the international limelight, which too often exposes the immaturity of young conductors and causes irreparable damage to their careers.

Though the Ulm theatre was tiny, that did not prevent Karajan from putting on such major productions as Wagner's *Die Meistersinger* or Strauss' *Salome.* In fact, Karajan con-ducted six different operas every year in Ulm and, at the same time, studied six more for performance the following year. He also conducted operetta and concerts as part of

9

his duties.

During the summers away from Ulm, Karajan was gaining equally valuable experience in Salzburg, attending the Festival events, and later becoming a rehearsal coach. It was here that he came under the influence of the great stage director Max Reinhardt. When Karajan later began producing most of the operas he conducted in the early 1950s, it was Reinhardt's name and memory he invoked most often.

It was also during this time that Karajan was exposed to perhaps the most important musical influence of his life — Arturo Toscanini. He had first heard Toscanini conducting *Lucia* and *Falstaff* with the La Scala ensemble in Vienna. This event marked a turning point in his development.

Neither opera had been done in Vienna for a long time, and *Lucia* was known to Karajan only from his study of it for piano. He had always considered the music banal, but in Toscanini's hands, it was transformed altogether. Suddenly it was filled with beautiful melody! From this experience Karajan discovered how a melody that appears to be quite ordinary on paper could be made to sound beautiful with only the slightest change in detail. Though Karajan has since developed a wonderfully acute ear for the subtle adjustment of melodic detail, at the time the transformation Toscanini had achieved seemed miraculous.

After that Karajan attended every Toscanini performance he could manage, including the concerts with the New York Philharmonic on its first European tour under Toscanini in 1930, and his rehearsals and performances in Salzburg. He even rode his bicycle from Salzburg to Bayreuth, a distance of more than 250 miles, to hear Toscanini conduct *Tannhaeuser* in 1931.

Since Salzburg, with its renowned performances constantly reminding him of what was lacking in Ulm, Karajan conducted what he describes as being "two" orchestras — the real one and an ideal one in his head.

But Karajan stayed on in Ulm year after year. At a time

when life in Germany was becoming particularly oppressive, when enormously high unemployment and Hitler's Third Reich were rapidly taking complete control, Karajan had very little choice. However unsatisfactory Ulm was, his chances for employment elsewhere were not good.

Eventually though, whether he liked it or not, he was forced to seek another job. After five years at Ulm he was suddenly fired. Only later did Karajan discover that the Intendant did it for Karajan's own good. The Intendant feared Karajan would be stuck in Ulm and never get out.

In the long run, Karajan obviously benefitted from this unconventional and drastic way of promoting his career. In the short run, however, it was another story. At the age of 25, Karajan suddenly found himself on the street, with no engagements in sight, and would spend many sleepless and hungry nights before he found another job.

Karajan left Ulm with many fond memories of his performances, among them *Die Meistersinger*, *Lohengrin*, *Fidelio*, the Beethoven Third Symphony, the Mozart D Minor Piano Concerto, in which he occupied the dual role of conductor and soloist, and a special Strauss evening with an enlarged orchestra of 90 players in *Don Juan* and *Ein Heldenleben*. But memories were of little practical value to him now. During his last year in Ulm he spent most of his time travelling throughout Germany looking for a job, without gaining even a single audition.

Just when he had almost given up hope, he was granted an audition for a vacancy at the Aachen Theatre, a prospect that nearly failed because the players in the orchestra considered him too young.

Aachen was certainly a step up from Ulm. At the Aachen Theatre Karajan could work with an orchestra of 70 men rather than 20 odd, and a chorus of 300. And, before he had been in Aachen a year he was appointed *Kapellmeister*, or musical director. With that appointment Karajan became, at 27, the youngest *Kapellmeister* in Germany.

11

This was really Karajan's first important post. He had a good orchestra at his disposal and could engage the finest singers and soloists. It was here that he conducted Wagner's *Ring* cycle for the first time. On the basis of the reputation he was making in Aachen, he was soon invited to appear in all the important musical centres of Europe, including Vienna and Berlin.

Since Karajan took up his new post in Aachen in 1934, one wonders how much soul-searching was involved. 1933 had been the year of the infamous Reichstag fire that brought the Nazis to power. It was also the year in which Bruno Walter was prevented by the Nazis from fulfilling engagements in Leipzig and Berlin and forced to leave Germany. So also, within the year, had gone Klemperer, Kleiber, Fritz Busch and Thomas Mann, among others. At the very moment Karajan was seeking work, Hindemith's opera *Mathis der Maler*, was banned by the Nazis, prompting Furtwaengler to resign all his permanent posts and to go into retirement for a time.

Whether he liked it or not, it was certainly obvious to Karajan that politics had suddenly become very much involved with art. To become Kapellmeister in Aachen in 1935 Karajan was required to join the Nazi Party, which he did. As Winthrop Sargeant revealed in an interview with Karajan in 1961, Karajan's decision was made entirely for opportunistic reasons, as Karajan himself admits: "I would have committed any crime to get that post." (*New Yorker*, December 2, 1967) Though Karajan could hardly be classed as a war criminal — then or later on — he could not fail to recognize as a musician that Germany had been taken over by a fascist regime of the most repressive sort. Conductors were forbidden to play works by Jewish composers such as Mendelssohn, Mahler, or Schoenberg. Orchestras were not allowed to retain their Jewish members. In addition, it became customary to play the Horst Wessel song, the Nazi anthem, before concerts and to give the Nazi salute if

12

officials were in the audience.

Why did a man like Karajan, who was notoriously uncompromising about almost everything, endure such indignities? Why did he not resist like Furtwaengler, who protected the Jewish members of the Berlin Philharmonic? It must be remembered that Furtwaengler was in a special position. He was the very symbol of cultural normalcy in Germany, and the Nazis would have suffered his opposition, whereas a less important international celebrity such as Karajan would have been rendered unemployable had he protested.

Karajan, moreover, saw an opportunity to advance his own career and took it. Like Furtwaengler, he doubtless deplored Nazi interference in musical affairs, and hoped for the Nazis' early demise. But, in spite of the political events that had overtaken Germany, cultural life during the Third Reich was extremely rich. In Aachen and later in Berlin, Karajan was able to work under conditions of which he could only dream during his years in Ulm. The Nazi leaders were extremely generous toward the arts so long as they maintained a fairly rigid conservatism, and Goering, who had special responsibility for the Berlin State Opera where Karajan was to spend so much of his time, allowed him considerable autonomy.

Furthermore, it can be argued that it was not the Nazis but the people of Germany who profitted most from the continued activity of Karajan and Furtwaengler. As many said after the war, they simply lived from one concert or opera to the next, for that was the only time during their wretched existence when life had any spiritual quality: music represented for them the sole remaining shred of humanity and dignity.

In 1937 Karajan appeared at the Vienna State Opera for the first time, conducting Wagner's *Tristan und Isolde* at the invitation of Bruno Walter. It was a great triumph for Karajan and must have been especially satisfying for him to return as conductor to the opera house in which he had

13

learned so much as a student ten years before.

Karajan was appalled, however, by the conditions under which a conductor had to work in Vienna. In fact he was so shocked at what went on that he nearly walked out. The general rehearsal promised him was cancelled, and at the ensemble rehearsal the leading singers in the cast sang only a few notes and spent the rest of the time catching up on their private correspondence. Karajan was therefore forced to make his debut in Vienna with virtually no rehearsal at all. Unfortunately, the situation was no better when Karajan took over the Vienna State Opera in 1956; during his nearly eight years there he was to fight a losing battle against such conditions.

After his initial success in Vienna Karajan was offered a permanent appointment, which he declined. He much preferred to work under the conditions he enjoyed in Aachen. There he did not have to fight for rehearsals. Better to be number one in Aachen than number two or three in Vienna, as far as he was concerned.

Karajan derived satisfaction both from his work and his personal life in Aachen. He had a small house in the woods near the city, which he occupied with his wife, Elmy Holgerloef, the first operetta singer of the Aachen Theatre whom he married in 1938. Unfortunately, however, the marriage could not withstand the pressures of Karajan's career and ambition, which necessitated his commuting regularly between Aachen and Berlin, and the marriage ended after three years.

As early as 1937 Karajan had been invited to conduct the Berlin Philharmonic. He declined this first invitation, however, since he had been offered no rehearsal time. The following year the Philharmonic was prepared to meet his terms, and he conducted his first concert with the orchestra in 1938. His program comprised Mozart's *Haffner* Symphony, Ravel's *Daphnis and Cloe* Suite no. 2, and Brahms' Fourth Symphony.

Karajan astonished the orchestra by asking for section rehearsals. First he wanted to rehearse the strings alone; then bring in the rest of the orchestra. The players of the august Berlin Philharmonic couldn't believe that the 29-year-old conductor from Aachen was serious. After all, they had been playing these pieces for years and thought they knew them better than he did. But Karajan persisted, getting the violas to play difficult passages on their own, and, when they got into trouble, practising it in a slower tempo first. As one might imagine, the orchestra members were not particularly enamoured of Karajan, but they respected him. For his part, Karajan loved the orchestra from the moment he set to work with them.

During Furtwaengler's lifetime, however, a closer relationship between Karajan and the Berlin Philharmonic was not possible. The Nazis seemed to have deliberately set Karajan and Furtwaengler against each other in an attempt to diminish the older conductor's stature. Thus, from the time Karajan first appeared at the Berlin State Opera in 1938 and received the famous "Das Wunder Karajan" review, about which more will be said later, Furtwaengler could not very easily invite Karajan to conduct the Berlin Philharmonic without undermining his own increasingly untenable position. Even after the war, things did not improve; and as long as Furtwaengler headed the Vienna and the Berlin orchestras, Karajan was unable to get near either one.

By the time Karajan was invited to conduct at the Berlin State Opera in 1938, the opera house — the most important in Germany — had lost most of its first-class conductors. Furtwaengler had refused to conduct there after the *Mathis der Maler* incident in 1934, and his successor, Clemens Krauss, had since left for a post in Munich. Despite the fact that the Intendant, Heinz Tietjen, was notoriously abrasive with conductors, Karajan characteristically insisted on his own terms. According to Ernst Hauesserman in his book, *Herbert von Karajan Biographie* (Bertelsmann Sach-buchverlag, Guetersloh, 1968), when Tietjen, through his secretary, offered Karajan a performance of a new opera by Wagner-Regeny called the *Burger of Calais* and sent Karajan a score to look at, Karajan studied the score and replied that he would be happy to conduct the opera, as long as he could also conduct *Fidelio*, *Tristan*, and *Die Meistersinger* — with adequate rehearsal time.

Tietjen's man considered this to be out of the question, but suggested that Karajan could possibly conduct *Carmen* with the "best casting." "What do you mean by 'best cast-ing'?", Karajan retorted. Then came the cast list. Karajan wrote back that this was not what he understood by "best casting," that the Wagner and Beethoven operas were "out of the question," and that he must decline the invitation to conduct at the Berlin State Opera.

This reply dropped like a bomb. It was tantamount to saying to Tietjen "I will not conduct for you." Next came a handwritten letter from Tietjen himself in which he offered Karajan *Tannhaeuser*. Karajan wrote back: "There must be some mistake. I don't wish to conduct *Tannhaeu-ser*, but rather *Fidelio*, *Tristan* and *Die Meistersinger*."

Finally, Tietjen gave in, and Karajan made his debut at the Berlin State Opera on September 30, 1938 conducting *Fidelio*. Before Christmas he had conducted *Tristan* and a new production of the *Magic Flute* as well. He also con-ducted the *Burger of Calais* early in 1939.

It was only after his first rehearsal at the opera house that Karajan met Tietjen face to face for the first time. "So you are a great meteor," Tietjen said. When Karajan began to say something, Tietjen cut him off: "Don't say anything. Conduct again as you did just now. I have heard your rehearsal and we need not talk any more about these things."

Karajan soon established himself as the most exciting conductor to hit Berlin in years. After his performance of

16

*Tristan* the critic van der Nuell referred to him as *"Das Wunder Karajan"* and suggested that some older conductors could learn something from him. Furtwaengler, naturally, took this as a personal affront and protested to the authorities. Later, during Furtwaengler's denazification proceedings, there was some evidence to suggest that van der Nuell had been put up to the extravagant Karajan review by Furtwaengler's enemies in the Nazi hierarchy. In any case, this certainly cast a shadow on the famous *Das Wunder Karajan* review.

With or without van der Nuell, however, Karajan became very popular in Berlin, and in November 1939 accepted the post of *Staatskapellmeister* at the Berlin State Opera. In addition, he revived the *Staatskapelle* concerts, which used to be given by the opera orchestra. The Berlin Philharmonic was denied him on a regular basis by Furtwaengler, but he enjoyed some great successes with this orchestra and made a number of recordings with them.

In fact, Karajan spent so much time in Berlin and other great European musical centres that the authorities in Aachen were disturbed. Finally, in 1941, he gave up his post in Aachen to concentrate on his work in Berlin.

While Karajan was away from Berlin on a conducting tour, he read in the paper that Furtwaengler had conducted a special concert for the Berlin State Opera House, which had been quickly rebuilt after being severely damaged by bombs. With Furtwaengler's return to the opera Karajan had immediately become *persona non grata*. Tietjen explained this was simply a matter of higher politics: the Nazi officials who backed Furtwaengler had apparently gained the ascendancy over those who backed Karajan. Another explanation is that Furtwaengler simply could not tolerate Karajan after the *Das Wunder Karajan* incident.

In any case, shortly after that, Karajan was ordered to report to the army. With the help of his dentist's daughter, who was Goebbels' secretary, Karajan succeeded in having

17

the order rescinded. After 1941, however, the only concerts he conducted in Berlin were with the *Staatskapelle*.

Karajan's career definitely flourished during the Third Reich. With the departure from the country of so many first-class conductors, the young Karajan had numerous opportunities he might not otherwise have had. But his career certainly suffered severe setbacks from 1941 onwards.

Karajan had established himself as a remarkable young conductor in pre-war Berlin. His practice of conducting everything from memory, including whole operas, his performances of baroque music conducted from the harpsichord in eighteenth-century style, his trance-like behaviour on the podium, all made him a figure worth watching. Had his conducting career been terminated at that point, it is doubtful whether he would be held in the esteem he is today. Some considered his interpretations too flashy and too brutal, in a word, immature. In an interview published in *The Saturday Review*, October 26, 1963, Karajan himself seemed to agree:

> As a young conductor I had many faults. For one thing I was always hurrying the tempo of everything I conducted. People tried to tell me this, but I wouldn't listen to them. When I finally began to study my recordings, I realized they were right. Today when I hear these early records, I feel I must have been drunk when making them!

Some would go so far as to say that the first signs of the new, mature Karajan did not come until 1961, in a particularly warm and human performance of *Tristan* at the Vienna State Opera.

Whether or not that is a fair judgement we shall try to determine later. Nearly everyone would agree, however, that it is the post-war Karajan who took Europe and the world by storm and who established himself as a major conductor.

18

# 2
# After the War

Like so many German artists after the war, Karajan was prevented by the Allied authorities from conducting until his name was cleared. Moreover, German artists remained unwelcome in many countries for years after their official denazification. In the United States, for example, a campaign was launched in 1948 to prevent Furtwaengler from coming to Chicago; even as late as 1955 the New York Musician's Union nearly succeeded in preventing Karajan from appearing with the Berlin Philharmonic.

Karajan, towards the end of the war, had retreated to Italy and semi-retirement. Though he was able, at war's end, to arrange the occasional engagement in Italy, he was prohibited from conducting in Austria and Germany with the exception of one concert he conducted in Vienna with the Vienna Philharmonic in January 1946. The invitation extended to him to conduct Mozart's *Marriage of Figaro* and Strauss' *Der Rosenkavalier* in the summer of that same year was also withdrawn at the last moment, at the insistence of the Russians.

The man responsible for persuading the authorities to ease their restrictions on Karajan was Walter Legge, at that time director of artists and repertoire for EMI in England. Shortly after the war, Legge, coming across a wartime recording of Karajan conducting the *Fledermaus* Overture,

19

was so impressed that he set out not only to sign Karajan to an EMI contract but also to obtain official permission for him to record. And so, from October to December 1947, there followed a series of recordings with Karajan and the Vienna Philharmonic, including Beethoven's Eighth and Ninth Symphonies, Schubert's Ninth Symphony, the Brahms' *Requiem*, and a host of other pieces. It was these recordings that gave Karajan the international exposure he so desperately needed after the war to reassert himself as an important conductor. The long apprenticeship in Ulm and Aachen, the fame at the Berlin State Opera, these credentials now counted for nothing and were best left unmentioned.

The 1947 recordings, which, unfortunately, have long been deleted from the catalogue, represent an important first step in Karajan's meteoric rise to prominence in the post-war years. One of the most memorable, the Brahms' *German Requiem* with soloists Elisabeth Schwarzkopf and Hans Hotter, has earned the praise of even some of Karajan's most outspoken critics. However, my own choice as the best recording from the 1947 sessions would be Schubert's Ninth Symphony. Though Karajan recorded the work again in 1971 with the Berlin Philharmonic, in a rendition that was highly praised for its drive and power, the later version seems positively insensitive in comparison to the earlier: for one thing, the tempo of the slow movement is nearly doubled in the later recording as though Karajan had grown impatient with the length of the movement; for another, the brutality of the fortissimos is truly shocking.

Of the Beethoven, Strauss and Mozart recordings made during the same period one can only say that they are free of eccentricity and that they display all the virtues of the Vienna Philharmonic. As interpretations, however, they do not compare, I feel, with those of Toscanini, Furtwaengler, or Walter.

Once Karajan was officially denazified, he quickly be-

20

came a dominant force in post-war European musical life. In 1949 he began working regularly at Milan's La Scala. Soon Karajan headed La Scala's German section — conducting most of the company's repertoire and eventually producing operas as well. It was here that he carried out almost all of his operatic work until his appointment to the Vienna *Staatsoper* in 1956.

Karajan held very firm beliefs about opera production. For a long time he had been of the opinion that only a conductor was capable of successfully staging operas — especially, in his words, works "of the highest symbolic meaning" such as those of Wagner. When he did finally begin to produce and light his own productions, Karajan encountered frequent criticism, particularly for his seeming preference for gloom on stage. When Rudolf Bing, for example, was told of the number of lighting rehearsals required for a Karajan production in Vienna, he was heard to remark: "I could have got it that dark in one rehearsal." Later, however, when Karajan came to work at the Met and won the respect of its technical staff, Bing was singing an altogether different tune: "Karajan," he said, "was unquestionably the outstanding artistic phenomenon of my latter years at the Metropolitan."

Although Karajan's productions at La Scala numbered no more than one or two per year, each was meticulously prepared in the characteristic Karajan manner, with months of rehearsal. This is not to say, however, that the productions were not sometimes tinged with absurdity, as in the 1953 presentation of *Lohengrin* in which the principals in the cast sang in German and the chorus in Italian, since the latter hadn't had time to learn the work in German.

One of the outstanding Karajan productions in 1953 was the world premiere of Carl Orff's scenic drama *Trionfo d'Afrodite*, starring Elisabeth Schwarzkopf and Nicolai Gedda, who was hailed as Karajan's "new tenor discovery."

In 1954 at La Scala, Karajan conducted Donizetti's

*Lucia di Lammermoor,* with Maria Callas in the title role. It was a great success, and the first of many collaborations between Callas and Karajan. In 1955 the entire *Lucia* production was taken to Berlin for two performances, one of which was broadcast and is now available on the private Limited Edition label. And just as Toscanini had done in Karajan's student days, Karajan took *Lucia* on tour to the Vienna State Opera in 1956, on the eve of his appointment as artistic director in Vienna.

During his years of close affiliation with La Scala, Karajan recorded two operas — *Il Trovatore* and *Madame Butterfly* — both of which feature Maria Callas and both of which reveal his genuine affinity for Italian opera — an affinity that few of his German or Austrian colleagues share. Because of the radical stylistic difference between nineteenth-century Italian opera, with its extrovert passion and obsession with virtuosity, and the German tradition, which turns on Wagner, few conductors are at home in both worlds; fewer still excel in both. Over the years Karajan stands nearly alone as a conductor highly praised for his Wagner — but praised also for his Verdi and Puccini. Many critics considered his *Ring* cycle performed in Salzburg from 1967 to '70 to be musically the best of our generation. His *La Bohème*, too, has been hailed as a landmark wherever it has been performed — in La Scala, Moscow, or Montreal.

Some may argue that the Callas recordings of the middle-fifties leave something to be desired: Di Stefano, for example, in the de Sabata recording of *Tosca* from the same period, was in much better voice. And the sound is rather boxy even by the prevailing standards of the day. Some would go so far as to say that Karajan was more efficient than inspired, rounding off the vulgar edges of these scores where he should have revelled in the excesses. But this is to quibble about various possible interpretations of the operas, any of which could be justified. If any criticism is to be made of Karajan it cannot be on stylistic grounds; it

22

is a question, rather, of differences of taste or temperament. Since Karajan is not by nature vulgar, undisciplined or sentimental, the listener cannot realistically expect to find these qualities in an Italian opera he conducts. That side of Italian opera is very real, to be sure, but Karajan is not interested in stressing it; as any artist, he must try to enhance what he considers to be a work's "good" qualities and obscure its "bad" ones.

Occasionally, during the period 1949 to 1956, Karajan left La Scala to conduct elsewhere, most notably at the Bayreuth Festival in 1951 and again in 1952. This festival, founded by Wagner for the performance of his own music dramas and held in a superb auditorium designed to the composer's specifications, has as its outstanding feature a covered orchestra pit that allows a perfect balance to be achieved between singers and orchestra. Over the years Bayreuth has set new standards for opera production, and nearly every Wagner conductor of distinction has made his mark there, including Furtwaengler and Toscanini.

When Karajan came to Bayreuth he was, at the age of forty-three, extraordinarily young to be put in charge of the complete *Ring* and *Die Meistersinger* one year and *Tristan und Isolde* the next, but he quickly made his mark as the most important Wagner conductor to emerge since the war. His performance of *Die Meistersinger*, recorded live at Bayreuth and issued commercially, still stands today as the standard by which all other performances of the work are judged. In the eyes of many critics this particular performance contains a freshness and an exuberance that are altogether lacking from the later version Karajan made in Dresden in 1971. This is, in all probability, due to the fact that the Bayreuth version is a live performance. But the quality of singing on the later recording is also variable. Theo Adam as Sachs is strained to the limits of his resources; René Kollo as Walther seems to have great potential but is not really at home in the part. The 1974-75 Salzburg Easter

23

Festival production with Karl Ridderbusch as Sachs and the Berlin Philharmonic in the pit more nearly approximated the Karajan ideal.

Had Karajan not been convinced that he must produce Wagner's music dramas himself, he might still be at Bayreuth. But Wagner's grandsons, Wieland and Wolfgang, who headed the Bayreuth festival in the early 1950s, were reluctant to hand over the production end of the operation to Karajan — especially Wieland, who was making a name for himself as a producer. Since Karajan had already begun to produce as well as conduct at La Scala, he would not agree to restrict himself only to conducting at Bayreuth. It was perhaps inevitable that the greatest Wagner producer and the greatest Wagner conductor of our time would go their separate ways, but for those who witnessed their joint productions in 1951 and 1952 it was a tragedy. The *Tristan* production of 1952 especially struck many observers as the most perfect realisation of the work they had ever witnessed. Later, after Karajan stormed out of the Vienna State Opera in 1964, there was some negotiation between Bayreuth and Karajan, but it came to nothing. Had Karajan not had the option of beginning a new festival in Salzburg he might have been lured back to Bayreuth. But his Wagner in Salzburg, as we shall see in a later chapter, was successful enough to silence even the most nostalgic who would like to see him back in Bayreuth. In any case, Wieland Wagner is now dead, and no successor of stature has as yet emerged.

*Karajan and the Philharmonia*

During the immediate post-war period Karajan was also active as a symphony conductor with the Philharmonia of London and the Vienna Symphony. His affiliation with the former arose out of his association with Walter Legge,

24

director of artists and repertoire for EMI. Shortly after his series of recordings with the Vienna Philharmonic in 1947, Legge, who had the foresight to see that the recording industry was going to boom after the war, founded the Philharmonia Orchestra in London, mainly for the purpose of recording. Record buyers everywhere were eager for discs by the great European artists, which had been denied them since the outbreak of war. Legge, who realized that an international corporation like EMI would do well to have its own orchestra, had in mind something like the NBC Symphony, which had been created by the National Broadcasting Company expressly for Toscanini and brought together the best players it could find.

Legge managed to assemble a fine group of players. What remained was to make an orchestra out of the men; for this purpose he turned to Karajan. Legge was already familiar with Karajan's achievements in the light of the Vienna recording sessions and believed him to be the best conductor of the post-war generation. Through 1948 Karajan conducted endless rehearsals with the orchestra and began to make recordings with it. Already, in London in 1947, Karajan had conducted the orchestra for the concerto debut of the Rumanian pianist Dinu Lipatti, and it was with Lipatti that he made one of his first Philharmonia recordings. In April of 1948, with Lipatti and the Philharmonia, he recorded the Schumann Concerto, which remains one of the outstanding recordings of the work. Subsequently Karajan made a number of recordings with the orchestra — all of the Beethoven symphonies, a whole series of major operas including *Cosi fan Tutte, Falstaff, Ariadne auf Naxos, Hansel and Gretel, Der Rosenkavalier* and *Die Fledermaus*, and dozens of orchestral showpieces. Throughout the early years of LPs Karajan and the Philharmonia were an ubiquitous combination.

Yet, while their records sold very well and Karajan's name quickly became known internationally, Karajan was

25

still not accepted everywhere as a major conductor. When he brought the Philharmonia to New York in 1955 the orchestra was greeted with great enthusiasm, but Karajan himself was accorded a much cooler sort of acclaim. Efficient, yes, but lacking in excitement and temperament. The situation was much the same in London, and, what is more, Karajan was not much better known to English audiences than to North American ones. The Philharmonia gave very few public concerts in those days and Karajan conducted only one or two a year. When he did appear in public he was criticized for the shallowness of his approach; he was a man interested in the effects he could draw from an orchestra rather than in the service he could render the composer. His recordings with the Philharmonia tend to confirm this judgement. The orchestra always plays well; there is hardly ever any willful interpretative distortion, but often nothing much happens either. The most memorable Philharmonia recordings under Karajan are perhaps those he made with such soloists as Gieseking and Lipatti. The Grieg Concerto with Gieseking and the Schumann with Lipatti have a range of expression and poetic insight conspicuous by their absence in other Karajan recordings of the period. There were, of course, other fine recordings: the series of operas with Schwarzkopf, for example. These were pioneering efforts in the pre-stereo days — first-class Mozart and Richard Strauss recordings with excellent casts. But even in such an acclaimed recording as *Der Rosenkavalier*, Karajan's work is more often virtuoso than profound. And in the Beethoven symphonies he recorded with the Philharmonia, speed is often substituted for insight. At his worst Karajan is efficient, cold, and boring as in the recordings he made of the Mozart symphonies or of *Falstaff*, which has almost none of the exuberance essential to the work.

But, to be fair, some of these shortcomings are more properly due to the *quality* of the EMI recordings, which made Karajan and the Philharmonia sound rather cold and

26

neutral. The bass lacks body and is always rather thin; the inner parts in the strings and winds never seem to achieve their proper effect; and the timpani sound is nearly always too light, if not inaudible. A case in point is Beethoven's Ninth Symphony. If one listens with score in hand one cannot be sure that the timpanist is playing in the first movement. In the scherzo, on the other hand, the engineers seem to have taken special pains to give it prominence — just the sort of prominence, in fact, the timpani should have had in the first movement. The *Missa Solemnis* recording however, probably stands alone as the worst EMI ever produced for Karajan and the Philharmonia. The choral sound is fuzzy throughout the work, and the combined sound of chorus and orchestra in the loud passages is often nothing more than incomprehensible noise. Only the outline of Karajan's interpretation comes across. Very poor quality for a recording made about 1958!

Although Karajan and the Philharmonia made many recordings from 1948 to 1960 and went on a number of important tours, the Philharmonia was never, in any real sense, *his* orchestra; nor did Karajan try to make it so. During this period his best work was being done elsewhere: in opera, at La Scala; in the concert hall, with the Vienna Symphony and, later on, with the Berlin Philharmonic.

Karajan's last concert with the Philharmonia was given on April 2, 1960, in a program comprising Bach's Suite no. 2 with flautist Gareth Morris as soloist, Strauss' *Death and Transfiguration*, and Schumann's Symphony No. 4. Of the Strauss work the *Times* critic commented: "It was a blazing, overwhelming interpretation that would be hard to equal."

*Karajan in Vienna*

Immediately after the war Karajan appeared with the Vienna Philharmonic in Vienna and Salzburg — conducting perfor-

27

mances and later making recordings with the orchestra. Prior to the war he had grown accustomed to working with Berlin's finest ensembles, including the Berlin Philharmonic. It was this type of orchestra that mattered most to Karajan and it was this type of orchestra with which he could work most successfully. What threw his plans and dreams into disarray, however, were the paranoia and intransigence of Furtwaengler. From the time of Furtwaengler's restoration to power in 1948 to the time of his death in 1954, Karajan was simply not invited to such major centres as Vienna, Berlin and Salzburg. Later, it became obvious that it was Furtwaengler who was responsible for this state of affairs. At this time, however, because of the uncritical adulation of Furtwaengler that prevailed in Vienna and because of the arrogance that Karajan projected to the public, the latter was frequently accused of Machiavellian scheming. While Karajan was director of the Vienna State Opera, for example, the press reported that he had tried to prevent a concert in Vienna by Wolfgang Sawallisch "by every means at his disposal." Many people, without a shred of evidence to go on, were quite prepared to believe this kind of statement. A strong reply, however, came from Walter Legge, a friend of both Karajan and Sawallisch. He revealed that Karajan had, in fact, gone to great lengths to get Sawallisch to accept the invitation. Legge went on to comment on the Furtwaengler-Karajan relationship as he, personally, had experienced it:

> It was my misfortune to be the principal buffer between Dr. Furtwaengler and von Karajan from 1946 until Furtwaengler's death. Karajan's stoical fortitude in those years was a model of long-suffering patience; not even his closest friends ever heard a word of comment from him. His only comment was "the old man is making his own life hell. But he is teaching me that the only way to enjoy eminence is to encourage and help one's colleagues." That is what von Karajan is doing now. [*Musical Courier*, July 1957]

Karajan had, in fact, gone out of his way to help several

28

younger colleagues: at his insistence, Mehta, Abbado, Ozawa, and Muti were invited to Salzburg. Nevertheless, the rumour still persists that Karajan has been instrumental in preventing Barenboim from recording with the Berlin Philharmonic, even though the orchestra is very agreeable to the idea.

Though prevented by Furtwaengler in the early 1950s from conducting the Philharmonic and the *Staatsoper* in Vienna, Karajan remained a force to be reckoned with. He was appointed "conductor-for-life" of the Vienna *Singverein*, one of the bulwarks of Viennese musical life for more than a century; he was also named conductor of the city's second orchestra, the Vienna Symphony. Neither of these ensembles was anything to "write home about" when Karajan took them over. But Karajan, according to a close observer, H.C. Robbins Landon, managed to transform the *Singverein* from an undisciplined group, which usually made noises more suitable to a beer hall than a concert hall, into a first-class chorus. The same kind of transformation was also achieved with the Vienna Symphony, whose concerts soon came to rival those of the Philharmonic. Karajan appeared annually in a series of concerts with the orchestra known as the *"Karajan Zyklus"*.

Curious though it may seem, the musical life of Vienna appears to have been greatly enlivened by the rivalry between Karajan and Furtwaengler — a welcome relief since the war had made it difficult to attract artists of the first rank. In a dispatch for *Musical America* in 1951 Max Graf described the situation:

The concert public has benefitted by this rivalry. It overwhelms Mr. Furtwaengler with applause and applauds Mr. von Karajan with equal enthusiasm. Vienna is still Vienna; it has lost none of its capacity to split into groups which feud and intrigue, just as in the days when the adherents of Brahms and Bruckner warred openly and partisans drove Gustav Mahler from his position as director of the opera. [*Musical America*, December 15, 1951]

29

As it turned out Karajan soon took his turn under the lash of Viennese intrigue. His eight years as director of the Opera (1956-64) featured one crisis after another. And, like Mahler, he too was finally driven from the house. But that will be recounted in a later chapter.

The Philharmonia and the Vienna Symphony were, in actual fact, surrogate orchestras for Karajan: the former, useful as a means of making recordings that would earn him recognition and money; the latter, as a means of maintaining his presence in Vienna and persuading the public that he was every bit as good as Furtwaengler. With the death of Furtwaengler, and, as a result, gaining access to both the Vienna and Berlin Philharmonic, Karajan left the Vienna Symphony and reduced his work with the Philharmonia to a trickle until he finally ceased to appear with it altogether.

By this time, the Philharmonia had a superb reputation, and was highly appreciated by both Furtwaengler and Toscanini. Why then did Karajan leave behind an orchestra of this quality? The fact is that for all its unquestionable excellence the Philharmonia could not begin to give Karajan what the Berlin or the Vienna Philharmonic had to offer. The Philharmonia was a purely commercial undertaking; as long as its records sold well and there was enough recording and film work to do, the orchestra could survive. By contrast, both of the European orchestras (the Berlin and Vienna Philharmonic) because they received subsidy, were guaranteed adequate rehearsal arrangements, no outside commercial work, and a security that ensured the highest artistic standards. Another drawback of the Philharmonia was that it gave only a few concerts, which meant that Karajan was unable to work with the orchestra over an extended period of time. It simply could not give Karajan the conditions he needed to realize his own artistic dreams.

Long after he left the orchestra, when asked if he would ever return to conduct it, Karajan replied characteristically, saying that he didn't know the players and they didn't know him and that the results of that kind of collaboration weren't of much value to anyone. In a way he was quite wrong, of course. Guest conductors often stimulate orchestras to play as they never played before, and conductors frequently find it a great challenge to win over a new orchestra. Karajan himself obviously had this in mind when he agreed to be Musical Counsellor of the Orchestre de Paris a few years ago. But it is true that he finds it less and less satisfying artistically to do guest conducting and has done very little since about 1960.

Even before he took over the Berlin Philharmonic in 1955, Karajan was considered an important conductor in Europe; he was also a source of fascination to those who had witnessed his trance-like state on the podium or to those who know of his sports cars and flamboyant way of life. If all that had survived from this period had been his recordings with the Philharmonia, Karajan might not have been considered a major conductor. For him, these were still formative years during which he was shaping his post-war image. The great conductor emerges only after the death of Furtwaengler when Karajan becomes director of the Berlin Philharmonic at the age of forty-six.

# 3
# Berlin Philharmonic

Whether in the concert hall, the opera house, or the recording studio almost all of Karajan's works these days is done
with the Berlin Philharmonic, the orchestra to which he
was appointed conductor-for-life in 1955. Under Karajan's
baton, in addition to performing over sixty concerts each
year in Berlin and on tour in Europe, Japan and North
America, the orchestra plays for the opera Karajan produces
at the Salzburg Easter Festival. Moreover, the vast majority
of Karajan's recordings in recent years have been made with
this orchestra. After more than twenty years of performing
together, Karajan and the Berlin Philharmonic have established an extremely close working relationship and have
profound respect for one another.

The Berlin Philharmonic, founded in 1882, is one of the
younger great orchestras of the world, compared to the
Vienna Philharmonic, the Leipzig *Gewandhaus*, the Boston
Symphony, founded one year before, or the New York
Philharmonic, which dates back to 1842. The first permanent conductor of the Berlin orchestra was Hans von Buelow,
the friend and leading interpreter of Wagner and Brahms.
It was Buelow who married Franz Liszt's daughter and had
the singular misfortune to see her elope with Wagner. But,
being the musician he was, Buelow did not let this development cast a shadow over his good relations with Wagner.

Buelow had the distinction of conducting the premiere of *Tristan und Isolde* in 1865 and was considered the greatest conductor of the day, especially in the light of his concerts with the famed Meiningen Orchestra, a crack group of just forty-eight players who performed standing up and were able to play most of the standard repertoire by heart. It was also Buelow, as legend would have it, who put on black gloves to conduct the Funeral March of Beethoven's *Eroica* Symphony.

The conductor who succeeded Buelow in 1895 as head of the Berlin Philharmonic was Artur Nikisch, a former violinist who had played under such composers as Wagner and Brahms. After Buelow, he was one of the first to direct all performances from memory. He was also one of the first great conductors to make recordings. Nikisch guided the destiny of the Berlin Philharmonic for twenty-seven years and was succeeded in turn by Wilhelm Furtwaengler.

While Nikisch, when conducting, was renowned for his clarity of beat and severe physical restraint, Furtwaengler baffled players by thrashing and bobbing all over the podium. In their approach to interpretation, too, Nikisch and Furtwaengler were poles apart. Nikisch was of an analytical bent, while Furtwaengler sought to bring out the poetic content in the music and relied a great deal on the inspiration of the moment.

It was Furtwaengler who had the unpleasant task of guiding the Berlin Philharmonic through the Hitler years. Though he was vilified for remaining in Germany, he is credited with saving the lives of many musicians, including some Jewish players in the Berlin Philharmonic.

During the period after the war, when Furtwaengler was prevented by the Allied occupation forces from conducting the Berlin Philharmonic, the orchestra was headed by the young Rumanian conductor, Sergiu Celibidache. But, once he was officially denazified, Furtwaengler took up his old post with the orchestra and held it until his death in 1954.

Furtwaengler died almost on the eve of the orchestra's first tour to the United States. In desperation the orchestra players went to Karajan and asked him to take over. He agreed, but only on condition that he be appointed Furtwaengler's successor. The orchestra members, while on tour, voted for Karajan to assume this position.

Naturally, it was difficult for Karajan to try to fill Furtwaengler's shoes, but not so difficult as some today would have us believe. The fact is that Furtwaengler was far from well in his later years. He had become increasingly deaf, so much so, in fact, that the Siemens Company had to wire the podium for sound in order that he might hear the orchestra. And, in his personal and professional relations with the orchestra, he was a difficult person to get along with: he had become absolutely paranoic about other conductors threatening his own power and was notorious for repeating musical phrases over and over until the players were exhausted.

Karajan very quickly asserted his authority over the orchestra and used his charisma to enhance the orchestra's reputation. While he certainly improved the orchestra in terms of the type of players he attracted and the precision he demanded, Karajan was probably just as much changed by the orchestra. Already in his early recordings with the orchestra in the mid-fifties, one notices a warmth and expressiveness that are totally absent from the Philharmonia recordings. Undoubtedly the tradition of the Berlin Philharmonic, nurtured by Buelow, Nikisch, and Furtwaengler, deepened Karajan's interpretative maturity. But this is not to say that he modelled himself on any of them: the Toscanini of the 1930s was an earlier, more powerful influence. But Karajan probably owes more to Furtwaengler than is generally recognized. Since all three conductors of the Berlin Philharmonic in the twentieth century — Nikisch, Furtwaengler and Karajan — recorded Beethoven's Fifth Symphony with the orchestra, a comparison of their interpretations offers a unique insight into the distinctiveness of Karajan's interpretation and his accomplishments with the orchestra.

Such a comparison of the Nikisch, (DG 2721070) Furt-waengler, (Heliodor HS 25078) and Karajan (DG 138804) interpretations is, of course, hampered considerably by the purely sonic differences of the recordings, but there is, nonetheless, much to be learned.

The sound available to Nikisch in 1913, and even to Furtwaengler in 1946, is far inferior to that afforded Karajan in 1962. One can scarcely speculate, for example, about Nikisch's dynamic range or his ear for balance and texture on the basis of his recording of the Beethoven Fifth. (Toscanini, in fact, claimed, that this recording was a total misrepresentation of Nikisch.) But there are other features of the Nikisch performance that are reasonably clear. First of all it can be distinguished from the other two in that it omits the repeat of the exposition or first part of the movement. This is an unusual practice, which certainly up-sets the clear-cut structure of the movement, and may have been only for the purposes of recording. However, apart from that, one notices very early on that the basic tempo is quite deliberate; rather slow, in fact. But — and this is important when one subsequently turns to Furtwaengler — there is only one basic tempo in the performance. Nikisch speeds up and slows down from time to time, but only very slightly for the most part. The most obvious exception is the phrase that the horn intones several times in the move-ment to introduce the lyrical second subject. Each time it occurs Nikisch gives the individual notes special emphasis, a somewhat mannered interpretation to *our* ears. Notice also how Nikisch spins out the little oboe cadenza, and how he holds the last enunciation of the motto theme forever. One begins to think it will never end.

The Furtwaengler performance does have certain features in common with the Nikisch. Furtwaengler, too, interprets the various tempo and dynamic markings in the score rather more freely than we are accustomed to today: like Nikisch, for example, he wrings every last ounce of meaning from the little oboe candenza. But, unlike Nikisch, Furtwaengler employs three basic tempos for the movement — disrupting the flow of the music as few conductors have dared to do before or since. There is one very slow, weighty tempo for the motto theme every time it appears; a second very quick tempo for the fugato passage based on the motto; and a third for the lyrical second subject, introduced by the horn figure that is so lovingly dramatized by Nikisch. Furtwaengler plays the horn figure in a fairly straightforward fashion but the same cannot be said for what follows.

Furtwaengler takes all these liberties; yet Beethoven has indicated only one tempo for the movement: *allegro con brio*. Intellectually, one is appalled by what Furtwaengler does, and the players of the Berlin Philharmonic seem to be having great difficulty adjusting to the tempo changes. Emotionally, however, the effect is quite different. Furtwaengler produces a performance of astonishing spontaneity and intensity, which leads us to suggest that he was perhaps violating the letter of the score in order to get at the spirit of it.

Also worth noting in Furtwaengler's performance of the first movement is the very long silent pause near the end, after the great climax of the movement. It is a momentous silence, as important to the music as the notes themselves. Once again, however, there is no justification for it in the score: Beethoven has not indicated any rests or silent beats.

Karajan, unlike Nikisch or Furtwaengler, had at his disposal the very best in modern stereo sound. There is a dynamic range and a clarity of texture in his recording of the symphony, that was not available to the other two conductors. In addition, he was able to benefit from the most sophisticated editing techniques, which can eliminate the slightest imperfection in performance.

The Furtwaengler recording was a live performance but, even so, a very messy one; and the Nikisch recording was probably made under unimaginable conditions. As for Karajan's performance, it is clearly in the Toscanini tradition. It follows faithfully every marking in the score and proceeds at an extremely fast pace. Again, like Toscanini and *unlike* Nikisch or Furtwaengler, Karajan maintains one basic tempo. Though he does relax slightly for the second subject and does give special emphasis to the motto theme when it is hammered out by the trumpets and timpani at the climax, the overall impression is one of driving motor energy. The oboe cadenza is not drawn out as it is by Nikisch and Furtwaengler, and there are no exaggerated holds or pauses. It is, in short, a literal performance of what Beethoven actually wrote.

But, like Toscanini, Karajan demonstrates that a literal performance need not lack either expressiveness or excitement. In the *fortissimo* sections, the Berlin trumpets are wonderfully full and golden. In the quiet passages the strings make a beautiful sound. The orchestra is under control at all times. Furtwaengler made an epic mini-drama out of this movement; Karajan settles for a purely musical *tour de force*. Both interpretations reveal an important aspect of the real Beethoven, and it would be meaningless to choose between them — any more than one could choose, say, between Gielgud's or Olivier's *Hamlet*.

But Toscanini's influence on Karajan should not be overstated. Never is a Karajan performance characterized by the speed and aggressiveness that so often made Toscanini's performances seem overwrought. In the slow movement of his recording of the Fifth Symphony, Karajan is closer to Furtwaengler in his lingering over expressive phrases, especially in the winds. And if one compares the three conductors' interpretations of the *Ring*, Karajan's similarity to Furtwaengler is even more striking. Both

37

conductors favour broad tempos and a long line, whereas Toscanini opts for forward motion and more marked contrasts in mood. Some would say that Karajan, since taking over the Berlin Philharmonic, has become more like Furtwaengler; others that he has simply become more self-indulgent or narcissistic. Personally, I prefer to think that Karajan has matured and that he has become mindful of his European roots.

While this has given many of his performances a new dimension, it has also proved to be a definite liability. In 1963 Karajan's recording with the Berlin Philharmonic of Stravinsky's ballet score *Le Sacre du Printemps* promptly incurred the wrath of the composer, who reviewed the recording, along with two others of the same work, in the American magazine *Hi-Fi Stereo Review*. Stravinsky's general criticism of the Karajan performance was that it was too polished for the nature of the music: in keeping with the subject of the work and the composer's intentions, it ought have been more primitive and savage. In Stravinsky's words:

> The *sostenuto* style is the principal fault; the note lengths are virtually the same here as they would be in Wagner or Brahms, which dampens the energy of the music and leaves what rhythmic articulation there is sounding labored. [*Hi-Fi Stereo Review*, October 1964]

While it is true that Karajan's performance is polished, and that he tends to tone down some of the savagery of the music, Karajan does adhere to the letter of the score for the most part, and his performance of *Le Sacre* is not without power, beauty, and logic. This, however, raises an interesting problem: is it possible to praise a performance of a work that the composer himself dislikes? Many composers have been quite prepared to learn from interpreters of their music. When Gieseking began a Rachmaninnoff piano concerto about five times more slowly than the composer himself ever played it, Rachmaninoff, who was in

38

the audience, couldn't have been more pleased. Not all composers are as dogmatic as Stravinsky.

Whatever one thinks of the results a conductor gets from an orchestra, it is always fascinating to find out *how* he gets those results. In rehearsal the conductor is often far more sympathetic (or despicable) than one imagines from seeing him wave his arms about in the course of a public performance. His task is to persuade the players to accept his interpretation of a piece and to encourage them to perform it as best they can.

Rehearsal records featuring conductors such as Toscanini, Furtwaengler, Walter, Beecham, Jochum, and Boehm have been available from time to time, and any serious and determined student of music will be able to find a way of attending the rehearsals of nearly any conductor who interests him. In all probability, his time will be better spent there than in listening to the average conducting teacher. Presuming a certain level of overall musicianship, the basic techniques of conducting can generally be learned in about half an hour and one really becomes a conductor only by practising and observing the great conductors in rehearsal. The secret of conducting is not what a man does in the performance — for by that time it is usually too late to do anything very useful; rather, it is what the conductor was able to accomplish in rehearsal. Thus, if we really want to understand Karajan we must go to his rehearsals. Unfortunately, that is all but impossible. A Karajan rehearsal takes place in halls as closely guarded as Fort Knox. But the record companies have given us a glimpse of Karajan in rehearsal. A few years ago Deutsche Grammophon released a recording of Karajan rehearsing the Beethoven Ninth Symphony with the Berlin Philharmonic. And, more recently, EMI issued (although only in Europe) a set of recordings of Karajan rehearsing the last six Mozart symphonies.

One's initial impression of these rehearsals is, as one of the Berlin Philharmonic players put it, "of a whirlwind", for Karajan works very quickly and attends to the tiniest detail.

Obviously the Berlin Philharmonic has played these pieces more times than it cares to remember. How then can such strenuous and meticulous rehearsing be required? The answer is that, like any orchestra, the Berlin Philharmonic easily falls into a routine, especially with familiar repertoire. It is the conductor's duty to make sure that this never happens. During the rehearsal of a familiar work he must let the orchestra know that they cannot afford to take it easy; he does this by being extremely attentive to every note and nuance in the playing. Karajan is a master of this kind of sensitivity, as the rehearsal recordings make perfectly clear.

Those familiar with Karajan's high standards and his impatience with incompetence might imagine that he rules the Berlin Philharmonic like a dictator. This is not at all true. In nearly every respect, Karajan is *primus inter pares* — no more. This means, for example, that it is not up to him to choose the orchestra players. Candidates for positions play before the whole orchestra, whereupon each member of the orchestra casts his vote; Karajan can only veto the orchestra's choice. Each new player is then put on probation for one or two years, after which the voting procedure may be repeated.

At rehearsals Karajan rarely raises his voice; he is never rude to individual players. How then does he achieve such good results? The answer is that he is respected as a musician and the players know that he is giving a great deal of himself. It is that simple.

The Irish flautist James Galway, who has been a principal in the Berlin Philharmonic for a number of years, is, generally speaking, not a man who likes to be pushed around. In fact, he has no use for most conductors. But Karajan and the Berlin Philharmonic are quite unique:

40

To play in the Berlin Philharmonic is like being in heaven. Everybody in our orchestra can really play and they have something to say individually. And of course collectively the whole orchestra really goes. There's no such thing as a routine concert. For example, recently we gave a children's concert in Berlin and Karajan rehearsed the Dvorak G Major Symphony which we've played together a million times, as if it were the most important concert in our career.

I find that Karajan is a very ordinary man. You go and talk to him and it's just like talking to my Dad. I can say exactly what I want to and he will give me a straight answer. Karajan is the greatest conductor alive today in my opinion. I can't think of an instance where I came off the platform with Karajan and thought, "Well, that was routine." Every time I play with that guy it's just the greatest. [In conversation with author]

Each summer, for some years now, the *crème de la crème* of the orchestra went to Karajan's home in St. Moritz to make recordings and to have a kind of working vacation. It was here that Karajan and the orchestra recorded Mozart Wind Concerti and Divertimenti and Handel Concerti Grossi, and works for small orchestra by other composers. Between recording sessions Karajan and the orchestra would climb mountains or go bowling or swimming. It was a charming change of pace — for conductor and orchestra alike.

After more than twenty years with the Berlin Philharmonic Karajan regards it almost as his own instrument, and plays on it as a great violinist plays on his Stradivarius. There is a very personal, intimate musical relationship between them: he has absolute respect for the players, and they, in turn, have tremendous confidence in him. They may, possibly, disagree with some of his interpretations — this player abhors his approach to Mozart, that one dislikes his Beethoven — but virtually all of them marvel at his knowledge of a score and his ability to get exactly what he wants from them. (One player told me that he had never played a real *pianissimo* until he played under Karajan.) But the players do not feel that he restricts their artistic expression; rather, he establishes a discipline that enables them to give even more of themselves.

The players in the Berlin Philharmonic think highly of Karajan for both artistic and economic reasons. They credit Karajan not only for maintaining the present high standards of the orchestra, but also for obtaining for them a very large sum of money through increased sales of records bearing his name. Royalties from the recordings provide the players with an additional sixty percent above their regular salaries, which are comparable to those of most other orchestras in the world. Thus, without Karajan the players in the Berlin Philharmonic would be appreciably poorer.

But that does not preclude strong criticisms of Karajan's interpretations by some orchestra members. When, on one occasion I was talking with two violinists from the orchestra and asked them about Karajan's Beethoven, one made a horrible face; the other volunteered that his Beethoven had improved a great deal in recent years. While the first man insisted that Karajan's reading of the *Pastorale* was still as bad as ever, the second felt that Karajan was now concerned with more than speed and impressive dynamic contrast in Beethoven, and that he was moving in the direction of Furtwaengler. However, this kind of criticism takes place in every orchestra with respect to every conductor. Players, after all, are not necessarily the best judges of a conductor's interpretations. They are too involved with their own problems as violinists, bassoonists, or cellists to have a really balanced view.

As for the suggestion that Karajan's trances and beautiful gestures are intended as much for the audience as for the orchestra, the players regard his style as very functional and as an incentive to commitment and concentration. This does not mean, however, that Karajan is not concerned with the audience. But his concentration encourages the audience to concentrate, and his beautiful gestures provide a useful clue to the structure and character of the music. Is it really preferable to have a man who is constantly pointing to the different instruments or jumping all over the place?

Many players in the orchestra have expressed the view that Wagner is the composer closest to Karajan's heart and that it is Wagner's music that draws the best out of him. In many respects the playing of the Berlin Philharmonic under Karajan at the Salzburg Easter Festival since 1967 has been the high point of their relationship.

In his concerts with the Berlin Philharmonic Karajan has always been very careful in his choice of soloists. Over the years he has tended to work with a small circle of performers with whom he feels comfortable. Among them are the pianists Christoph Eschenbach, Alexis Weissenberg, and, more recently, Jean-Bernard Pommier; violinist Christian Ferras; and cellists Pierre Fournier and Rostropovich. Some have said that he chooses to work with soloists whom he can bend to his will and that he avoids really strong personalities. There is some truth to this. Karajan does not want to work with musicians with ideas radically different from his own. But what conductor does? At the same time, he doesn't deliberately choose faceless talents. The names above certainly do not fall into this category, and second-rate performers would not do much for Karajan's reputation. The performers who do work with Karajan find their relationship with him very special. According to Weissenberg:

> He really brings out the best in all of us. His infectious personality is such that it is not that he changes your tempi or makes you do something very different. On the contrary, he lets every artist be animalistically, what he is, but he does bring that animal to its best status, rather than oppress it as many people imagine. [Interview with author, Fall, 1974]

Also, contrary to another myth that has developed, Karajan and his chosen soloists do not pour over scores and rehearse bar by bar, note by note. In fact, very often

43

their mutual understanding is such that they do not rehearse at all, even for a recording. Again, to quote Weissenberg:

> The Beethoven Fifth Piano Concerto was almost recorded in the studio without ever having rehearsed it before. And the Fourth Concerto we had played together at Salzburg before we recorded it but once in the studio we went straight through without a rehearsal.

The secret of Karajan's success is the close understanding that exists between Karajan and the Berlin Philharmonic and the empathy that Karajan feels with his soloists. It is very real and productive. To me, Weissenberg has never sounded better on records than with Karajan.

Karajan has often been criticized for his repertoire: too little contemporary music and too much repetition of the same pieces in the standard repertoire. It is true that Karajan has not championed present-day composers, and, for some, that is a serious matter. According to German composer Hans Werner Henze, conductors are remembered precisely because they encouraged the music of this composer or that composer. Toscanini, for example, played Verdi and Puccini when they were alive; Walter conducted Mahler; Kleiber played Alban Berg; and so on. But who are the composers Nikisch championed? Or Furtwaengler? Or Szell? Conductors can make their mark in other ways besides being associated with the music of a particular composer of their time. This is not to suggest that Karajan's interest in music stops with Debussy. He regularly plays Stravinsky and Bartok. (He has recorded the 1943 Concerto for Orchestra no less than three times!) And he recently recorded most of the major orchestral works of Schoenberg, Berg, and Webern. It was Karajan who gave the world premiere of Carl Orff's *De Temporum Fine Comoedia* at the 1973 Salzburg Festival. As Music Director of the Berlin Philharmonic he has instituted a series of twentieth-century music concerts in which the very latest music is presented every year and he always conducts at least one of the concerts in this series. Though he is obviously very sceptical about much of the music being written today, he is by no means turning his back on it. If he is not himself interested in a new piece, he will often hire someone else to do it who is.

As far as other composers are concerned, it can safely be said that Karajan's repertoire is as broad as that of any other major conductor. It includes Mozart, Haydn, Bach, Handel, Beethoven, Brahms, Bruckner, Mendelssohn, Schumann, Strauss — virtually the whole German repertoire — the Sibelius symphonies, Shostakovich, Debussy, Berlioz and much else besides. He has his favourites, of course, and they do tend to show up on his programs over and over again: the Beethoven Fourth Symphony, the Bruckner Eighth, Strauss's *Ein Heldenleben*, Berlioz's *Symphonie Fantastique*, the Dvorak Eighth and a few others. But in these works he has become supreme; moreover he seems to be able to find something new in nearly every performance of them. To hear him conduct such works is a rare experience. Would we really prefer to hear him conduct the Saint-Saens symphonies, *The Pines of Rome*, or *Conflatus II* by "Stockhenze?"

There *are* some curiosities in his repertoire. For example, he is very fond of playing Mozart Divertimenti with the Berlin Philharmonic. For these works, which were probably designed to be played by solo string players (and two horns), he uses a whole string section. On principle I do not really like the idea; what sounds pure and clean played by one violin is apt to sound laboured and messy with seven or eight. One reason Karajan uses the string section, no doubt, is to challenge his string players and, hopefully, show them off. But what he achieves is much more than that. On records, his performances of K. 287 and 334 are correct but rather on the cool side. In concert, however, I have heard him produce electrifying results. The Berlin Philharmonic strings tear into the music as if their lives depended

45

on it, pouring out sumptuous tone while maintaining an astonishing lightness. Tempos for the quick movements are breathless but exhilarating; the slow movements are so sublime that time seems to stand still. Anyone who criticizes Karajan's Mozart for being cold and faceless has probably heard only his recordings. The concert performances of the Mozart Divertimenti have been moving and joyous experiences.

What strikes me again and again about the Karajan-Berlin Philharmonic collaboration is that, in spite of the detailed preparation that obviously precedes every performance and the exacting standards Karajan sets, there is, in contrast to what many critics seem to imply, nothing mechanical about the performances. On the contrary, there is a quality of abandon about them that altogether belies the superficially controlled physical presence of Karajan himself. It is a remarkable phenomenon.

# 4
# The Vienna State Opera

The Vienna *Staatsoper*, or State Opera, has been one of the world's great opera houses for many years. Its director during the first decade of this century was Gustav Mahler; his successors included Richard Strauss, Bruno Walter, and Karl Boehm. In view of the opera's proud heritage it is not surprising that Karajan jumped at the chance to become its artistic director when the job was offered to him in 1956. But Karajan also knew that nearly all of his predecessors had been driven from the house by a fickle public, meddling government ministers, a hidebound bureaucracy, or a combination of the three. And while Karajan was at the time the most revered artistic personality in Vienna, he, too, ultimately succumbed to the perils of the situation. The Viennese are still arguing about the pluses and minuses of his years as director of the opera and are still trying to determine who is really to blame for the problems he encountered.

By the time Karajan took over the opera in 1956 its prestige had sunk to its lowest point since the war. Karajan's job was to restore that prestige, and to do this he was given sweeping powers. But whether they were sweeping enough soon became a matter of controversy. Karajan was acquainted with some of the less admirable customs of the house.

47

He had last appeared there at the invitation of Bruno Walter in 1937 and had conducted Wagner's *Tristan und Isolde* with virtually no rehearsal.

Karajan's next engagement at the opera house was not until 1956, when he conducted *Lucia* with the visiting La Scala ensemble. In between there was the war, of course, but also the rivalry with Furtwaengler and the feuding cliques, who often had excellent government connections. Because of this situation Karajan was effectively prevented from conducting both the Vienna Philharmonic and the Vienna State Opera during these years – except for EMI with the help of Walter Legge. During the early 1950s this company issued complete recordings of Mozart's *Marriage of Figaro* and the *Magic Flute*, both of which were conducted by Karajan and featured leading singers of the Vienna State Opera and the Vienna Philharmonic orchestra. The Karajan-conducted *Figaro* was none too well received when it first appeared. Many critics took special exception to the fast tempos, which seemed to allow for little poetry or expression. The *Magic Flute*, however, received much more favourable reviews.

Before the war, Karajan had been active as an opera conductor in Ulm, Aachen, and Berlin; from 1947 on he was very much involved with La Scala in Milan. In view of Karajan's increasing reputation, the Vienna State Opera, in the spring of 1956, offered him the job of director, which he accepted. It was two days after Karajan's fantastic success in Vienna conducting *Lucia*.

Karajan's problems were vast in number for standards at the house had sunk to an all-time low, and discipline of almost any kind had become a joke. Joseph Wechsberg, who has been writing about opera in Vienna for as long as I can remember, characterized the situation in devastating detail:

> Poor-to-middling repertory performance with spiritless conducting, second-rate singing, and no pretense of staging are the rule. Inexperienced singers are often hired, often after a brief inconclusive performance. Rehearsals are unpopular; the orchestra is often studded with substitutes; artists must often appear at shortest notice, with little chance to find out what is going on . . . Things reached a sad climax a month ago when, after the premiere of *Tannhaeuser*, the artist singing the title role was booed out and later chased around the opera house by irate opera-lovers. [*Saturday Review*, April 27, 1957]

Before he conducted a single performance Karajan put in months of preparatory work. When he did finally announce his proposals for restoring the prestige of the house, they were, predictably, radical. The main reason for the decline of standards, he contended, was the *stagione* or ensemble principle on which the opera had been run for decades. Under this system, a small group of leading singers were contracted for the whole season and sang the principal roles in all the operas — be they German, Italian, or French. In an age when international stars could jet from one opera house to another and when the public could hear the best performing artists on records, only a provincial house could cling to the *stagione* system.

Karajan, therefore, demolished the *stagione* system, to cries of outrage still heard to this day. In its place, he proposed a system whereby leading houses such as La Scala and Vienna would exchange their best productions. This would mean more idiomatic German productions for La Scala and more idiomatic Italian ones for Vienna. In addition, the Salzburg Festival and Vienna would enter into an agreement whereby the Festival productions would be transferred to Vienna in the fall. This would reduce costs for both, because they could divide the capital expenditure; it would also mean that Vienna would have performances of Festival standard. Furthermore, Karajan pledged to sign leading conductors to contracts of several months' duration and get rid of the second-rate *Kapellmeisters*.

49

Because of Karajan's good relations with both Salzburg and La Scala, the two exchange programs were spectacularly successful (although no Vienna productions went to La Scala). Soon after he became director, Karajan conducted a stunning performance of Verdi's *Otello* with Mario del Monaco and Renata Tebaldi in the leading roles, roles that would have been filled in the past, and not half so well, by members of the ensemble company. A recording, which was also made with the same principals, shows a Tebaldi as Desdemona less youthful than she ought to be and a Del Monaco tending to bellow rather too often, but otherwise both singers give fine performances. Aided and abetted by Decca recording producer John Culshaw, Karajan conducted an *Otello* of immense power and beauty. Though the original choice for the role of Iago was Ettore Bastianini, he had, as Culshaw revealed years later, knowledge neither of the role nor the opera and was replaced on short notice by Aldo Protti. Karajan's later performances of the work at Salzburg with Jon Vickers and Mirella Freni in the leading roles were much superior, and there he had the benefit of a better cast. In 1973, Karajan made a second recording of *Otello*, this time with the cast of the Salzburg production, but the superiority of the later version is much disputed. While Alan Rich of *New York* magazine pronounced it "overwhelming" and "the year's great operatic album," a view echoed by Verdi expert Andrew Porter in *Gramophone*, others such as Peter G. Davis in the *New York Times* spoke of the "uncharacteristically weak orchestral ensemble," and criticized Karajan's "patchwork view of the opera." David Hamilton writing in *High Fidelity* found it "much like other recent Karajan operatic recordings, executed with much finesse but very little rhythmic force and continuity." Obviously, all these views cannot be correct but the differences of opinion are interesting.

When Karajan first came to Vienna he had great plans and was portrayed as the man who could rescue Vienna from the intermidable bickering and bungling that had plagued it for years. But, at the end of his first year as artistic director, even a critic as pro-Karajan as Joseph Wechsberg was unimpressed:

> Everything he does is high-voltage but also missing in depth. When you hear the same opera performed under him several times, the dazzling effect seems to wear off in later performances and there remains a curious vacuum . . . As his own producer he was often erratic and amateurish. [*Opera Annual*, 1957]

Because of his innovations at the Vienna State Opera, Karajan was worshipped by some and vilified by others. Whenever he conducted there was never any doubt about the quality of the orchestra or the preparation that had gone into every aspect of the production. In the *Ring* cycle, in *Parsifal*, *Otello*, and especially *Pélleas and Mélisande*, Karajan scored tremendous personal successes that brought the Vienna State Opera international recognition. And, because of his work in Vienna, Karajan's potential as a conductor was taken more seriously. On the strength of Karajan's performance of *Tristan* in Vienna, Harold C. Schonberg compared him to Toscanini and Furtwaengler:

> Karajan displayed almost unbelievable control over the orchestra . . . what we have not heard hitherto was the warmth, the humanity that Karajan gave to the score . . . whatever the reason we are witnessing a profound, if slow, change in his conducting. [The *New York Times*, July 23, 1959]

The "new Karajan", evident in the recordings made during this period with the Vienna Philharmonic, shows a warmth and flexibility only rarely hinted at in the Philharmonia recordings. At the same time, however, other critics still saw signs of the "old Karajan." Harold Rosenthal of *Opera*, after attending a performance of *Fidelio* at La Scala in 1961, commented: "Karajan externalized the score to such an extent . . . that I left the theatre in a rage."

For all his personal triumphs in Vienna, Karajan, as artistic director of the *Staatsoper*, was having little effect.

51

On the nights when he was not conducting, standards were often as low as ever. Neither had he succeeded in attracting conductors of stature to the opera house. Some charged that the conductors preferred not to come rather than risk the inadequate rehearsal time that prevailed whenever Karajan was absent; others claimed that Karajan took so much time for his own rehearsals there simply wasn't enough for anyone else's. But the real cause of the difficulties lay in Karajan's commitments elsewhere. As well as being conductor-in-chief of the Berlin Philharmonic, Karajan continued to conduct in London and Milan and had even begun to conduct in America. In addition, he began to tour widely with the Vienna Philharmonic. Because he was absent for months at a time throughout the season, Karajan could not begin to assert the day-to-day authority that was necessary to run a major opera house.

The situation really began to deteriorate, however, when the technicians union went on strike in the fall of 1961, forcing the postponement of several new productions. For most of the season the house was in a state of chaos while a settlement was being worked out. When it finally was brought about, it was imposed by the government, and Karajan resigned in protest. His resignation was supported by the orchestra and virtually the entire personnel of the house, including the technicians themselves. Within a short time, the government backed down and accepted Karajan's solution, but only with the proviso that a co-director be appointed to assure administrative stability during his absence. The new co-director was to be Walter Schaefer, at the time head of the Stuttgart Opera. When Karajan returned to the house after a long absence to conduct a performance of *Aida*, he was accorded a hero's welcome. When he tried to begin the Prelude he was prevented from so doing by the applause, and flowers rained down from the upper galleries.

The first season that Karajan and Schaefer co-directed

was not a success. Karajan continued to be absent from Vienna for long periods, and Schaefer was still heavily involved in Stuttgart; instead of one absentee director, the Vienna Opera now had two. When Schaefer finally chose to remain in Stuttgart for 1963-64, Egon Hilbert took over as co-director.

Karajan and Hilbert never got along. There was trouble right from the beginning of the season with a new La Scala production of *La Bohème*. The Vienna union refused to accept the Italian prompter, who had been part of the production in Milan, whereas Karajan and the whole cast maintained that he was indispensable. The lines were drawn. The opera was eventually given, but with no prompter at all. Though Hilbert did support Karajan in this dispute, the latter was so annoyed in the months following that the two men scarcely spoke to one another. Reports of chaos at the opera were front-page news in Vienna all season long. Hilbert was apparently fond of usurping artistic responsibility when it was a question of engaging singers and conductors. As if this were not bad enough, he even had the temerity to schedule Karajan to conduct his own production of *Tannhaeuser* on the same night he was supposed to conduct a concert with the Berlin Philharmonic in Vienna — and the Berlin engagement had been arranged long before! What is more, to add insult to injury, Hilbert engaged another conductor to substitute for Karajan at the *Tannhaeuser* performance, without even asking Karajan's permission.

The constant strain of fighting with government ministers, unions, and co-directors was too much for Karajan. During his eight-year stay in Vienna he suffered several nervous collapses. Eventually, he resigned from the opera in a fury and vowed never to conduct in Austria again. For full details (at least from Karajan's point of view) of the difficulties he experienced in Vienna, the reader is referred to Ernst Hauesserman's biography of Karajan.

On leaving the Vienna State Opera in 1964, Karajan was prepared to wash his hands of his native Austria for good. But the directors of the Salzburg Festival offered him such attractive working conditions there that Karajan conceded, at least to the extent that he agreed to conduct in Salzburg every summer. Since that time, he has not set foot in the Vienna State Opera. (The most recent report has it that Karajan will be director of the Vienna Festival in 1977 and will conduct his Salzburg opera productions at the *Staatsoper*.)

After Karajan's departure the opera house returned to the doldrums once more, except for the occasional guest appearance by a Bernstein or a Karl Boehm. In spite of the fact that an agreement had been worked out whereby Karajan was to return to Vienna in 1972 to conduct the Salzburg Easter Festival's production of *Tristan*, politics and deep-seated bitterness once again intervened. Powerful figures in Vienna were pushing for a Bernstein-Visconti production of *Tristan* during the same season. At one point, both Karajan and Bernstein were vowing never to conduct in Vienna again.

When he left Vienna Karajan also terminated his contract with Decca records, which had recorded many of his productions with the Philharmonic and the Vienna State Opera. Instead, he chose to sign an exclusive contract with DGG, which stipulated that he would record only with the Berlin Philharmonic. In the years following, only a few Karajan recordings were made in Vienna; any further recordings there necessitated special and costly arrangements. Although this state of affairs virtually terminated Karajan's recordings of Italian opera, which he and Decca were so fond of doing in Vienna, happily, with the production of *La Bohème* in Berlin in 1973 and *Madame Butterfly* in 1974, Karajan and Decca were involved once again in Italian opera.

Karajan's obvious enthusiasm for Italian opera is one of

the most memorable features of his years in Vienna. Unlike many Central European conductors Karajan has a special love and affinity for the lusty, uncomplicated art of Italy and for the uninhibited Italian singing style. In the course of a discussion with Winthrop Sargeant of the *New Yorker*, Karajan explained why he was so fond of conducting Italian opera:

> Take *Tosca*, for example. It's like having a good, simple, rare hamburger for a change. Very wholesome. It contains elemental emotions and violence. The amount of energy you can expend in *Tosca* — why it corresponds to a murder, and the beauty of it is that you don't have to be hanged afterward. [*New Yorker*, January 7, 1961]

As it happens, Karajan made a recording of *Tosca* during his last years in Vienna; it is a superb rendition of the opera.

In looking back on Karajan's years in Vienna, one can only say that however much he succeeded as a conductor, (in many memorable performances and recordings of the period), he ultimately failed as director of the opera. And he failed not only because he was fighting against overwhelming odds, but also because he was Karajan; that is, a man obsessed with perfection and with his own personal vision. He was also a shy man, often remote in personal contacts and exceedingly irritated by administrative chores — clearly not the kind of man to head a major opera house. In such a position he could not help but make life miserable for many people, granted, but most of all, for himself. With all the administration and politicking to be done, he simply could not get on with his own work. It is the Rudolf Bings of this world — the non-musical, non-creative managers — who can make a go of such a job, not the Karajans. And yet without the imagination and artistic insight of the Karajans the job cannot really be done properly either. Perhaps co-directors are the best solution for Vienna, if two compatible and complementary personalities can be found. As for Karajan, he has taken the situation into his own hands and come up with an ingenious solution that seems to work admirably for him: he has, in effect, started his own opera house — with himself as sole conductor and his productions the only productions ever given. This is the new Salzburg Easter Festival where Karajan has conducted annually since 1967. If anything goes wrong, Karajan has only himself to blame.

In Salzburg, Karajan is really in his element, concerned mainly with his personal growth as a musician and the realization of his own artistic vision.

# 5
# The Salzburg Festivals

Karajan's association with the Salzburg Festival goes back to the days of his youth and his early training as a musician: Karajan was born in Salzburg and was twelve years old when the first Festival was given. Since that time it has become one of the best-known of all the numerous summer festivals that have sprung up in recent years, and there is hardly any musician of importance who has not performed there in the past thirty years.

Karajan was deeply influenced by the musicians he saw working in Salzburg during his youth. Above all, he was impressed by the high standards of performance that prevailed there. While still in his twenties he attended rehearsals by Toscanini, Furtwaengler, Bruno Walter, and Max Reinhardt, and later worked as a coach for the opera and theatre productions.

Prior to the war, Karajan conducted in Salzburg on only one occasion — and not a very important one at that — for a ballet version of Debussy's *Afternoon of a Faun*.

After the war he was invited to conduct *Rosenkavalier* and *Figaro* for the first Festival in 1946. But a week before the Festival opened, the Allied authorities prohibited him from conducting, and for reasons that have never been made clear, Karajan did not return to the Festival for many years. My own theory is that by the time Karajan was given a clean bill of health by the authorities, Furtwaengler had re-entered the picture at Salzburg, and, because of his important position there before the war, was naturally given pride of place and first choice of all opera productions. As in the case of the Berlin Philharmonic and the Vienna State Opera, Karajan simply had to wait until Furtwaengler's death in 1954 before any opportunity arose for him.

In March 1956 Karajan signed a four-year contract as artistic director of the Salzburg Festival and conducted shortly thereafter stunning and memorable productions of *Fidelio, Electra, Falstaff*, and *Don Carlos*. Though originally the Festival centred around the works of Mozart, Karajan succeeded in convincing the directors of the need for more ambitious operas, and a new opera house was built for this purpose. This was the *Grosse Festspielhaus*, designed to Karajan's own specifications. It opened with a Karajan production of *Der Rosenkavalier* in the summer of 1960.

Though there was some criticism that the new house was too large for Mozart productions, the sweeping 115-foot proscenium opening, the elaborate technical equipment, and the magnificent sound were all greatly admired. Subsequently, the *Grosse Festspielhaus* has been the scene of some of Salzburg's most successful productions, including Karajan's *Otello, Boris Godonov, Der Rosenkavalier*, and Karl Boehm's *Wozzeck*. The production of Mussorgsky's *Boris* caused a sensation during the 1965-67 seasons. Sung in Russian, with a good many Russian and Eastern European stars taking part, it included the Sofia Radio Chorus and Nicolai Ghiaurov, who scored an immense personal success in the title role. It was a lavish production which made full use of the gigantic *Festspielhaus* stage, especially in the numerous processions and crowd scenes — too lavish for those who preferred a starker realization of the Mussorgsky score.

Once the new *Grosse Festspielhaus* opened in 1960,

Karajan resigned as artistic director of the Salzburg Festival. Those who had been against the idea of a new house from the beginning were outraged now that it was being abandoned by the very man who had conceived it. But, as usual with a Karajan resignation, there was more to the story. In this case, there were two main problems. First, the Austrian government wished to televise the inauguration of the new house and the performance of *Der Rosenkavalier* conducted by Karajan. After all, they said, the Austrian people had put several millions of tax dollars into the new opera house, and they had a right to see what went on inside. Besides, many of them would never be able to afford a ticket to an actual Festival performance. But Karajan wouldn't hear of the idea on the grounds that television would distort the quality of the stage production. As it happened, Karajan shortly thereafter produced his own film of the production but refused to allow Austrian television to participate.

The other problem which led to Karajan's resignation was his desire to produce Verdi's *Il Trovatore*. For the Festival directors, this marked too much of a departure from tradition — Mozart and Richard Strauss would have been more acceptable. The directors' fear was that if Karajan continued, Salzburg would become an opera house like any other; when they offered resistance to his projects Karajan took his leave as artistic director.

Later, in 1964, when Karajan resigned from the Vienna State Opera, the Salzburg directors apparently changed their minds. Karajan was invited back to Salzburg and was even given *carte blanche*. This meant the new productions of *Il Trovatore* and of *Boris*. So successful were these productions that Karajan was completely vindicated. Moreover, the purposes and traditions of the Festival have not been drastically altered. The emphasis is still on Mozart, but there is now more room for special productions of other works. And, not only is it the opera repertoire that has undergone expansion: since Karajan's return, there has also been more contemporary music performed at the concerts. With houses sold out for nearly every event, conservative Salzburg could well afford to become more adventurous.

But Karajan was not satisfied even with his *carte blanche*. What he wanted to do more than anything was Wagner's *Ring* cycle, and he wanted to do it at Salzburg where the technical facilities were perfect. He could not do it, however, at the summer festival since he would be competing with the Wagner Festival at Bayreuth; this would not only be insulting but also self-defeating, since the two festivals would be vying for the same singers and there simply weren't enough first-rate Wagnerians to go around.

Karajan's solution was typically iconoclastic: he would start a new festival at Salzburg that would be held at another time of the year. The result was the Salzburg Easter Festival, begun in 1967, where Karajan has staged and conducted the *Ring, Die Meistersinger, Fidelio, Tristan,* and other operas. Karajan has, in effect, started his own opera house since no one but he conducts at the Easter Festival. During the one week of productions, usually one and perhaps two operas are performed, and two choral or symphony concerts as well. All are conducted by Karajan, and all played by the Berlin Philharmonic. It is a monumental one-man show quite without parallel in modern times.

Another interesting feature of the Festival is that a recording of each opera is made months before its performance. The recordings are then made available on cassettes to the cast for study, and autographed copies of the records are issued to subscribers during the Festival. The 1973 Festival was typical. It featured Wagner's *Das Rheingold* and *Tristan und Isolde*, produced, lighted and conducted by Karajan, a Beethoven concert, and a choral concert comprised of pieces by Mozart and Verdi. Each concert was also given two performances; all eight evenings of the festival were conducted by Karajan and given during a period of nine days.

Ticket prices range as high as sixty dollars for opera productions and thirty dollars for concerts — staggering prices by any reasonable standards. But what is more astonishing is that the revenue from ticket sales does not even begin to cover the cost of the Festival and that all the events are sold out by subscription more than a year in advance!

The cost of the Festival is not mere extravagance. Opera production anywhere is very expensive. But in Salzburg, not only is one offered what is perhaps the finest conductor and orchestra one is ever likely to hear (an expensive enough combination) but, in addition, opera productions that are mounted on a scale that no other opera house can begin to challenge. Whatever else one says about a Karajan performance, one cannot dispute the fact that it is meticulously prepared.

Festival tickets, as I mentioned, are sold on a subscription basis. Moreover, thirty percent of the subscribers are members of the *Vereines des Foerderer der Osterfestspiele*, patrons, if you will, who not only subscribe to one of the two cycles but who also pay about eighty dollars per person over and above the subscription fee. For this extra donation they receive a number of special privileges. First, they are presented with a new Karajan recording of a work being done at the Festival, autographed by the maestro and not available to the general public until a later date. (In past years patrons have received copies of the Karajan *Ring* cycle, and in 1973 they were given a recording of the *St. Matthew Passion* as performed at the 1972 Festival and recorded later by Deutsche Grammophon in a set that was unavailable to the public until the fall of 1973.) Patrons are also admitted to a concert rehearsal and have a unique opportunity — unavailable to the general public — to see Karajan and the Berlin Philharmonic at work. What they see, however, is not really a working rehearsal. To take the

61

1973 Festival as an example, Karajan and the orchestra played parts of Strauss' *Sinfonia Domestica*, a piece they had played together many times. Karajan stopped the orchestra only occasionally to attend to tiny details of phrasing and ensemble, and the whole rehearsal lasted only three-quarters of an hour. But it was enough like a rehearsal to satisfy the patrons and therefore to justify the idea.

The fact is that the Easter Festival is a frightfully expensive undertaking — it receives no government grant (though the local government provides a guarantee against losses), and it needs all the help it can get from wealthy patrons. What makes the Festival so expensive is that so few performances of each opera are given. An opera house can only begin to cover its costs if it can give numerous repeat performances of a work to pay back the enormous capital expenditures for rehearsals and sets. The only area then in which the Festival saves money is on the concerts by the Berlin Philharmonic, for these concerts are treated as part of the regular tours of the orchestra and are consequently financed through the West Berlin Senate. Given the astronomical prices, the number of performances, and the enormous demand for tickets, it is no wonder that attendance at the Festival is a status symbol and that the Festival attracts the most snobbish audience imaginable and keeps out the average music lover.

But, given Karajan's ambition, there seems to be no other solution, for he insists on working under optimum conditions, and such conditions exist only in Salzburg. The *Grosse Festspielhaus* is the best equipped opera house in the world in terms of technical facilities, projectors, lighting, and so on. Since it is not in regular use as an opera house, Karajan can rehearse for weeks right on the stage. In addition, he can use pre-recorded cassettes during rehearsals instead of a real orchestra, a practice absolutely forbidden by the musician's unions in North America. Finally, he can use his own orchestra, the Berlin Philharmonic, rather than the average second-rate opera orchestra. As czar of the Salzburg Easter Festival he has only to worry about his own productions and not about everybody else's as he did at the Vienna opera. Since these conditions are necessary for the realization of his artistic ambitions, the result is that only a very wealthy few ever get to see Karajan at his best. The democratization of the opera house is incompatible with Karajan's ideals — except, that is, through the medium of television, for which he has already taped a number of his opera productions.

The Karajan Salzburg productions are remarkably good. The orchestral playing is incomparable, and the singers, on the whole, are carefully chosen and fully prepared. Schneider-Siemssen's stage designs and Karajan's lighting invariably produce a wall-to-wall spectacle that is rivalled only by Cinerama.

But the productions are not beyond criticism. The very size of the stage, which facilitates spectacular scenic effects, makes audibility and communication a very serious problem for most singers. Nevertheless, this has been vigorously denied by some of Karajan's favourite performers, Karl Ridderbusch or Helga Dernesch, for example. The size of the stage, they argue, makes singing and acting on it a challenge: they have to work that much harder to communicate with each other and with the audience. As for audibility, in their experience Karajan controls the volume of the orchestra so carefully that there is never any problem. Miss Dernesch was even more diplomatic, claiming that it wasn't really for her to say, but only for a third person sitting in the audience. As such a person I found a great deal of *Tristan* to be quite puzzling; I could certainly see mouths opening and closing but was unable to hear anything for minutes at a time. Despite Karajan's reputation for a "chamber-music" approach to Wagner, in heavily scored passages in Salzburg the singers simply cannot be heard. Lili Chookasian, an American contralto who sang in

63

*Die Goetterdaemmerung*, even suggested that the house distorts the quality of the voices. Yet Karajan insists on placing his singers well back on the stage, even during extended solo passages. In *Tristan*, for example, Dernesch sang her "Liebestod" from almost fifty feet back on the stage. The visual effect was marvellous but the singer could not always be heard clearly, and sometimes not at all.

Yet the virtues of Karajan's Salzburg productions far outweigh the drawbacks, for only in Salzburg do the conditions exist that give rise to the most impressive Wagner productions of our generation. It is in Salzburg that Karajan is at his best. Karajan was born in Salzburg and it is here, no doubt, he will achieve his most important work in the years to come.

Of any aspect of the Salzburg festival the orchestra is, probably, its single most outstanding feature. Under Karajan the Berlin Philharmonic plays Wagner with an authority unequalled anywhere in the world, and it plays with unusual dedication and commitment, for Karajan demands not only technical perfection, but poetic insight from the first bar to the last. It is one of Karajan's outstanding qualities as a conductor that he can maintain tension in music like no other conductor can, whether it be a single melodic phrase, a scene, or a four- or five-hour opera. During a performance Karajan never relaxes. He may not appear to be doing much, and the music itself may be subdued, but close up one can see that his whole body is poised as though he were about to spring, and his face is taut and tense. In the repertoire Karajan has made his own — above all the Wagner music dramas — Karajan's work in Salzburg has set new standards for musical productions. The recordings, splendid as they are, capture only a small fraction of Karajan's achievement. The visual dimension and the extraordinary tension they are lacking can only be generated in live performances such as those one witnesses at Salzburg.

64

# 6
# Karajan in America

Unlike most leading conductors of his generation, Karajan did not appear in the United States until he was forty-seven; hence, well into maturity. Even today he is still a relatively infrequent visitor.

Karajan's involvement with American orchestras includes only two weeks with the New York Philharmonic in 1958, a few concerts with the Los Angeles Philharmonic at the Hollywood Bowl in 1959, two concerts with the Cleveland Orchestra in Europe in 1967, and a few appearances at the Metropolitan Opera in 1967 and 1968. Moreover, at a time when major American orchestras are desperate for musical directors, Karajan has turned down numerous offers in the United States.

In Europe, by contrast, Karajan has long had a reputation for accepting demands from a dozen places at once and, what is more surprising, for managing to meet the demands. (Karajan in a taxi: "Where to?" "Anywhere, they want me everywhere.") But for a variety of reasons, his involvement in American musical life came late in his career and it has never really taken root.

Undoubtedly Karajan's identification with the Third Reich and the stigma that remains from this association were partly to blame. Karajan's Nazi membership prompted a protest to the State Department in 1955 which nearly resulted in the cancellation of his debut in the United States; it probably also affected his negotiations with the Chicago Symphony in 1967. But there are undoubtedly other reasons for Karajan's infrequent visits to America, which most likely had more to do with the man himself and his artistic sensibility than with his critics.

In early 1955 the Berlin Philharmonic was scheduled to make its long-awaited debut in the United States under its famed conductor Wilhelm Furtwaengler. Since Furtwaengler, at no little personal risk to himself, had fought to preserve the traditions of the orchestra and to protect the lives of its non-Aryan players during the war years, and Berlin, with American help, had triumphed over a Russian blockade, the U.S. tour was intended to signify the triumph of German culture over Fascist and Communist challenges, and to show the gratefulness of the West German government to the American people.

But Furtwaengler did not live to bring the great orchestra to the United States: he died after a long illness on November 30, 1954. As a result, the American tour was in considerable jeopardy, for the orchestra's overseas passage had been guaranteed by Detroit industrialist Henry Reichold only if Furtwaengler were the conductor; with his death the offer was withdrawn. Fortunately, the West German government stepped in and agreed to subsidize the trip. The only problem was to find a conductor. Who could replace Furtwaengler? In the press the names of Herbert von Karajan and Sergiu Celibidache were bandied about, but it was clearly Karajan who had the inside track. Karajan had long had his heart set on inheriting the orchestra, and had gained a large following and powerful friends who might help him do so. When Karajan, a year before Furtwaengler's death, was approached by the orchestra manager, Dr. von Westermann, to see if he would take over the tour should anything happen to Furtwaengler, Karajan agreed, but only on the condition that he be appointed conductor-for-life of the orchestra. However, even after rehearsals for the tour had begun, Karajan had still not received any official word or any guarantee that he would succeed Furtwaengler, since the decision was up to the Berlin Senate, which could not meet until the tour was under way. The adamant Karajan would probably have withdrawn from the tour had the mayor of West Berlin not suggested a stop-gap measure: it was decided that, during a press conference heralding the departure of conductor and orchestra from Berlin, Karajan would be asked to succeed Furtwaengler by the senator in charge of culture. In this way, Karajan's succession was made public, if not yet official, and Karajan's pride was assuaged. It was not until the orchestra returned to Berlin after the tour that Karajan was *officially* appointed to succeed Furtwaengler.

But the difficulties that were to beset the tour had only begun. In the week preceding the orchestra's arrival at Idlewild, a wave of protests nearly succeeded in cancelling the tour altogether. A front-page story entitled "Musicians Oppose Concert Here by Nazi-led Berlin Orchestra" appeared in the *New York Times* of February 20, and 750 members of the American Federation of Musicians, Local 802 (New York) were circulating a petition that read in part:

> We musicians strenuously object to the appearance of the Nazi-led and Nazi-managed Berlin Philharmonic in New York. The conductor H. von Karajan, as well as the orchestra manager, was an active party member who bears responsibility for the death and exile of countless musicians from Hitler's Germany.

> We also protest the United States Government subsidy of this orchestra while American orchestras are denied such support. We urge you to prevent this performance.

Since it was standard practice at the time for the State Department to seek the approval of the American Federation of Musicians for any American appearances by foreign musicians (on the grounds that they threatened, theoretically at least, the livelihood of American musicians), this protest by the federation — quite apart from any moral or political considerations — seemed to be entirely justified. Unfortunately, however, the federation was mistaken about the facts: financial support for the tour had been provided entirely by the West German government, as the State Department was very quick to point out.

The other moral or political issue, however, was far less easily disposed of and plagued the orchestra and Karajan both during and after the tour. From February 8 until the opening of the tour in Washington on February 27, the *New York Times* ran almost daily reports on the rising crescendo of protest directed primarily at Karajan's wartime membership in the Nazi party. Almost to the very moment that Karajan lowered his baton at the first concert there was widespread doubt that the tour would go ahead as planned.

The day after the letter of protest from Local 802, the manager of the orchestra, Gerhard von Westerman, admitted his and Karajan's membership in the Nazi party but claimed that such membership had been purely formal: it had merely enabled them to continue their work in music. Unfortunately, such statements sounded too much like the excuses offered at Nuremberg and only served to fan the flames of outrage. The union denounced Westerman's explanation as "glib." By this time over 1,000 signatures had been collected from members of Local 802, and a petition was presented to the local's president Al Manuti. Moreover, the executive board of the local endorsed the protest and urged the federation to take whatever measures it could to "stop the tour under the leadership of these two men." But, much to the chagrin of the local, the tour had already been cleared by the federation, and James C. Petrillo, president of the A.F.M., declined to take a stand, claiming, "The decision is up to the State Department."

Although (judging by newspaper reports) they were few

in number, those who refused to go along with the protest movement were willing to say so in print. The American Committee for Cultural Freedom, for example, in a strong letter to Local 802 president Manuti, stated:

> The membership of von Karajan and von Westerman in the Nazi party over a decade ago, while deplorable, is not relevant to the non-political nature of the orchestra's appearance here.

At the same time the State Department, in a reply to the New York protestors that did not come until after the orchestra had begun its tour, pointed out that formal membership in the Nazi party did not in itself disqualify a person from being granted a visa to visit the U.S., and observed that the orchestra had met all legal requirements for admission to the United States. In the following weeks, however, it became a matter of some controversy that the relevant legislation, the Walter-McCarran Act, disqualified those who at one time or other had been members of a totalitarian (i.e., Communist) party from visiting the U.S., but seemed to exempt former Nazis.

By the time the orchestra arrived in the U.S. (on February 25) public interest was running high. Would there be demonstrations? If so, how serious would they be? There were, in fact, no pickets at either at the airport or the hotel, although they did materialize later at some of the concerts. What would Karajan say in his defense? Karajan merely made the statement, "I have nothing to say about politics, I come here as a musician." He then vanished from sight and didn't surface until the concert; his manager put out the story that he was suffering from a virus infection.

In the press the next day two long-time members of the Berlin Philharmonic defended their conductor and manager against charges or insinuations of pro-Nazi activities and sentiments. Both described how Westerman had protected them, their families, and other non-Aryan members of the orchestra from persecution, and had managed to continue to pay their salaries even after they had been dismissed by the Nazis.

The tour opened on schedule in Washington without incident. Moreover, since one of the prominent spectators at the opening concert was none other than Chief Justice Earl Warren, an important imprimatur from the American government was added to the tour. Karajan and the orchestra were rapturously acclaimed by both audience and press. In a program consisting of Mozart's *Haffner* Symphony, Strauss' *Till Eulenspiegel* and the Brahms' First Symphony, Karajan emerged especially triumphant. In the words of the *New York Times* critic, Jay Walz:

> Herr von Karajan, who gives the strongest impression while conducting of not having a bone in his body, somehow was able to make Mozart as fluid as it was precise. His Strauss score was as mobile as it was electric and the Brahms seemed to move with ease and naturalness to its broad, majestic sweeps. [February 28, 1955]

The only mishap that marred the concert was the Berliners' badly botched rendering of the American national anthem; in all the excitement that preceded the tour, someone had neglected to include the score. However, when Karajan returned to the United States in the fall for a tour with the Philharmonia of London, he was better prepared. William Walton, one of England's leading composers, had written an arrangement of the anthem for the orchestra.

On the day of the first New York concert, the State Department advised Local 802 of the American Federation of Musicians that the tour would go ahead, despite any opposition.

That evening 100 pickets outside Carnegie Hall carried signs reading "No Harmony with Nazis" and "They Helped Hitler Murder Millions." Inside, however, there was nothing but praise for conductor and orchestra. Howard Taubman of the *New York Times* captured the excitement of the occasion particulary well:

From the moment that the members of the orchestra began to file on the stage before starting time, the audience made known its amiable disposition. There were recurrent bursts of applause, which mounted in fervor as the concertmaster appeared, and they exploded into thunder when Herr von Karajan strode out. [March 2, 1955]

But, while generally praising Karajan and the orchestra, Taubman was particularly disturbed by the orchestra's lack of "light and sparkle" and remarked bluntly that "individual soloists in some cases do not compare with the best here and of some orchestras abroad." His remarks and those of others who heard the orchestra during this period remind us that Karajan did not inherit a perfect instrument. The Berlin Philharmonic's present exalted status is in large measure due to Karajan's achievements.

On March 3, at a press conference, Karajan finally faced reporters' questions, most of which, predictably, concerned his political views and activities during the war. He denied having any sympathy with the principles of national socialism. After a steady barrage of probing questions on the subject, Karajan's normally excellent English failed him, and his American manager, the late André Mertens, replied on his behalf. Apparently Karajan was not about to undergo interrogation on a subject that was obviously distasteful. Certainly nothing that he said or failed to say, however, satisfied those who were already hostile to him and the protests continued for the duration of the tour in Cincinnati, Baltimore, and the other cities where the orchestra played during the next few weeks.

Even after the orchestra's departure from New York, the pages of the *New York Times* carried on the controversy. In a long article entitled "Art and Politics," Howard Taubman tried to make some sense of the whole affair but refrained from issuing a verdict. He diplomatically made no mention of Karajan's name in the article and professed to understand everybody's feelings, while pointing out, somewhat meretriciously, how worthwhile it was for nations to exchange orchestras with one another.

On April 2, the day of the orchestra's departure from the United States, the *New York Times* carried a letter from one Irma E. Jaffe which indicated that feeling was still running high in some quarters:

> I say that we are not dealing with politics when we speak of nazism, but with morality — obscene morality — and a Nazi is one who chose an obscene morality to live by, or, at least, with . . . Let us not be deluded into a fake "political tolerance" — the issue here is morality.

But the protest probably reached its zenith on the occasion of the *second* Carnegie Hall concert, when a crowd of more than 500 gathered outside Carnegie Hall to protest the State Department's reading of the Walter-McCarran Act. Inside the hall three pigeons were let loose with protest messages attached to their legs but the disruption was limited to the occasional flapping of wings during quiet passages in the music.

Upon his departure from the United States, after a six-week reception that alternated between hostility and rapture, Karajan graciously expressed gratitude to the people of America for "their warm and friendly reception, which was above expectations." At the very least Karajan had succeeded in showing that if art was not entirely distinct from politics or morality, his own musicianship was beyond question and the heritage of the Berlin Philharmonic was in good hands. It must have been a very trying time for Karajan, for he was, in fact, in the process of proving himself on three fronts; to a public that was at least partially hostile; to an orchestra that was comparing him with Furtwaengler and was about to vote on him as permanent conductor; and, finally, to the senate of West Berlin, which would have the final say concerning his appointment and watched his every move to see if he was worthy — not only musically but also morally and politically — of becoming Furtwaengler's successor. Had Karajan been less in control of his words and actions on the tour, had the protests succeeded in cancelling the tour or seriously disrupting it, his appointment undoubtedly would have been jeopardized.

But Karajan did not have long to wait to learn the orchestra's intentions. On March 5 in Pittsburgh it was announced that a majority of the orchestra had voted for Karajan as their fourth permanent conductor. A few days after returning to Berlin his appointment was confirmed be the senate. To the formal question put to him by one of the senators, "Are you willing to lead the Philharmonic in the spirit of Furtwaengler?" Karajan replied, "with the greatest joy." Thus, the mantle of Wagner's friend Hans von Buelow, the legendary Nikisch, and the mystical Furtwaengler had fallen on Karajan.

The essential question, however, remained unresolved. Should Karajan be blamed for his one-time membership in the Nazi party? Local 802 thought so in 1955, and some of its members continued to think so in 1958 when Karajan was invited to conduct the New York Philharmonic. It is true that Karajan had returned to the United States without incident to conduct the Philharmonia of London in the fall of 1955 and the Berlin Philharmonic in 1956. But this was the first time that American musicians, many of them refugees from Nazi Germany or relatives of victims of Nazi persecution, would have to play for him. In any case, the members of the New York Philharmonic were notorious for their harsh treatment of conductors. (Many contend that they drove out Barbirolli in 1936 and took years off the life of Mitropoulos.) But, whatever else they were, the New York Philharmonic players were professionals. They played for Karajan, and they played without protest. What they did do, however, in a gesture that went unnoticed by many but was agreed upon in advance was to refuse to stand when Karajan came on stage, thus denying him the traditional gesture of respect granted to conductors. But Karajan, who was probably advised of this calculated af-

73

front, chose to let it pass. As it turned out, he was wise in doing so. His discipline won the day, and the orchestra played magnificently.

In programs which included the Strauss tone poem *Ein Heldenleben* and Beethoven's Ninth Symphony, both Karajan specialities, and with Leontyne Price (whom Karajan introduced to Europe) leading the solo quartet in the Ninth, Karajan conquered orchestra and audience alike. Howard Taubman of the *New York Times*, who was less than ecstatic about Karajan's interpretation of Mozart's *Jupiter* Symphony in the first program, found the Ninth quite another matter, for in it Karajan showed

> that he could conduct with tension and virility . . . this was for the most part Beethoven brimming with vitality and compassion . . . He has a fondness for lingering over poetic passages and tracing refined lines but he can also conduct with fire. [Nov. 22, 1958]

Once again Karajan had had to prove himself; as before, he emerged with flying colours.

In the summer of 1959, Karajan returned to North America for appearances at the Vancouver Festival and at the Hollywood Bowl. At this first international festival in Vancouver, Karajan, along with Bruno Walter, who gave one of his last public performances, was one of the star attractions. In an all-Beethoven program Karajan was well received but, according to some of the players involved, Karajan was not altogether happy with the experience. Although assured of a first-class orchestra especially assembled for the festival, Karajan found the players somewhat unresponsive during rehearsals.

At the Hollywood Bowl, leading the Los Angeles Philharmonic, he conducted two programs, one all-Beethoven program as in Vancouver, and one comprising old Karajan specialties, *Ein Heldenleben*, the *Meistersinger* Overture, the *Haffner* Symphony, and, rather surprisingly, Charles Ives' *Unanswered Question*. Karajan's control of the orchestra was duly acclaimed, but some found it a dubious virtue. Writing in *Musical America*, Albert Goldberg voiced some of the criticisms that have been directed at Karajan throughout his career:

> In all of Mr. Karajan's performances there was a curious repression and restraint. There was seldom any hint of abandon nor, for all the perfection of the playing, any pronounced excitement or emotional involvement. [August, 1959]

But strange as it may seem, after two series of concerts within nine months Karajan has never again appeared before an American orchestra in concert on American soil. (Of course, he did conduct the Met Orchestra in 1967 and 1968, but then only in the pit.)

And, though Karajan did conduct the Cleveland Orchestra in the summer of 1967, the concerts were given in Salzburg and in Lucerne, and not at Severance Hall in Cleveland. They were also the source of some controversy. Writing in the *Instrumentalist* in August 1968, Maurice Faulkner suggested that Karajan's erratic conducting technique very nearly caused the orchestra to break down during a performance of Prokofiev's Fifth Symphony:

> The beginning of the symphony started with ease and flexibility in the flutes and bassoon. Then the waving maestro closed his eyes and his difficulties began. Minute details such as delicate *pianissimos* and secondary motives were left to the discretion and interpretation of the musicians, who handled those aspects as brilliantly as is possible without much assistance from the podium. There were moments at tempo changes when the instrumentalists were at somewhat of a loss to learn of the maestro's intentions. But the *coup de grâce* struck the orchestra in the *adagio* third movement, during the *poco più animato* where the tonality modulates into F major and where the first violinists and cellists must pick up a motive in the most delicate *pianissimo*. Here the gifted concertmaster and his colleagues had to fathom the intentions of the change of mind of the conductor . . . with barely a noticeable slip in a couple of parts, the seam of the music was sewn up quickly . . . One of the instrumentalists, in describing his experiences under von Karajan, said, "We had to count bars like crazy!" [*The Instrumentalist*, August 1968]

75

Elsewhere in the press, a violist in the orchestra was quoted as saying that Karajan was more concerned with the audience than with the orchestra. All this would suggest that Karajan had a less than happy relationship with the Cleveland Orchestra but, in actual fact, he was invited to succeed George Szell after the latter's death in 1970. Karajan declined the offer on the grounds that his recent experience with the Orchestre de Paris had proven to him the impossibility of being musical director of two orchestras simultaneously, and, for him, the Berlin Philharmonic must always come first. Moreover, other musicians in the orchestra have told me that playing under Karajan was a wonderful experience.

Perhaps one explanation for the discrepancy might be that some players in the orchestra simply prefer a conductor like Szell who cued every important entry with his baton or his eyes; therefore, they felt insecure with one who seemed oblivious of them, for Karajan's technique is to thrash out problems in rehearsal and to concentrate on the music during the concert. Even in the Berlin Philharmonic, there are some players who would rather have more guidance during the performance than Karajan usually gives them. But the vast majority of those who are used to him appreciate the self-discipline and concentration he tries to encourage.

It is probably true to say that American musicians are more likely to be impatient with Karajan than their European counterparts and, similarly, Karajan with them. American orchestras generally have less rehearsal time so that the concert itself too often becomes another rehearsal in which the conductor is still needed to give cues for important entries and to show the players what to do. Since American orchestras do not enjoy the generous government subsidies of the Berlin Philharmonic or the Concertgebouw, they cannot afford additional rehearsals and must rely more on the conductor than might otherwise be the case.

Karajan rehearsing Mozart's *Coronation* Mass at the 1973 Salzburg
Festival, with soloists Gundula Janowitz, soprano, Brigitte Fassbaender,
contralto, Werner Krenn, tenor and the Berlin Philharmonic.
Photo: Lauterwasser

Karajan recording Bach's *St. Matthew Passion* for DG with baritone
Dietrich Fischer-Dieskau.   Photo: DG/Lauterwasser

Karajan and composer Carl Orff during rehearsals for the world
premiere of Orff's *De temporum fine comoedia*, held at the 1973
Salzburg Festival.   Photo: DG/Lauterwasser

Karajan and his wife Eliette leaving their house near Salzburg. Photo:
Ellinger

Karajan directs Mirella Freni (right) and Stefania Malagù (left) for his
Salzburg Festival production of Verdi's *Otello*.   Photo: Ellinger

*Tristan und Isolde* in the 1973 Salzburg Festival production by Karajan and Guenther Schneider-Siemssen.   Photo: Lauterwasser

Outside the Concert Hall: Karajan on a family outing and Karajan at the
controls of his airplane.   Photos: Ellinger

Curtain-calls at Salzburg for *Das Rheingold*. Left-to-right: Karajan,
Louis Hendrikx, Karl Ridderbusch, Brigitte Fassbaender, Leif Roar,
Hermin Esser, Jeanine Altmeyer. Photo: Ellinger

Karajan and the Berlin Philharmonic in concert at the Salzburg *Grosse
Festspielhaus*. Photo: Ellinger

A study in concentration.   Photo: Lauterwasser

Karajan long ago reached that stage of his career where he could insist on any number of rehearsals. With the Berlin Philharmonic he is able to program the same pieces over and over until every last detail has become second nature to both orchestra and conductor alike. Under these conditions, the Berlin Philharmonic does not need cues in the usual sense from Karajan, nor does Karajan have to preoccupy himself with giving them. Therefore, given the opportunity to achieve the kind of preparation and perfection he desires, why would Karajan expose himself to the less desirable conditions under which American orchestras work? In a recent interview, Karajan made it quite clear that he saw no point in guest conducting American orchestras, or those of any other country. In the November 1972 issue of *Gramophone*, Alan Blyth wrote:

> When I asked him if he would return to this country [England] to conduct for the New Philharmonia he replied that he couldn't do so because it would mean preparing something in too short a time. "Neither the orchestra nor the audience really gets much out of that. You must be entirely familiar with the works and the players."

Karajan did conduct American musicians again in New York, but only under special circumstances. In 1967 Karajan began his Salzburg Easter Festival. There he planned to produce and conduct Wagner's *Ring* cycle over a period of four years. But since the cost of preparing an opera for a few performances in Salzburg was staggering, Karajan came up with the idea of persuading other opera houses to borrow the production *in toto*, for an appropriate fee. As it turned out, only the Metropolitan Opera in New York was in the market for a new *Ring* and willing to meet most of Karajan's conditions. But Rudolf Bing, the general manager of the Met had been steering clear of him for years because feelings about Karajan over his Nazi past were still running high. By the mid-sixties, however, Bing realized that a conductor of Karajan's eminence — whatever his personal

77

history — was needed at the Met. Since he was looking for a new *Ring*, Karajan's approach to him was opportune. To make matters easier, Eastern Airlines donated $500,000 dollars, for, as Eastern's president Floyd D. Hall commented, "It's a good investment and good public relations." No doubt Karajan would have preferred to take the Berlin Philharmonic which had performed in Salzburg with him, but Rudolf Bing and Local 802 had other ideas. Thus, if the Salzburg project was to be properly financed, Karajan would have to abide by their wishes and be satisfied with the Metropolitan Opera Orchestra.

Once more Karajan was forced to make music with players who might well dislike him personally and to work under conditions he did not have to tolerate elsewhere. But according to Martin Mayer, Karajan need not have worried:

> The reaction of the Local 802 members at his first Met rehearsal on November 7 was no more than normally hostile, and at the performance the orchestra played better for Karajan than it has played for anyone else this season. The war has been over for twenty-two years. [*New York Times Magazine*, December 3, 1967]

Critical reaction to Karajan's conducting of *Die Walkuere*, however, was another matter. Most critics were bewildered by what came to be known as Karajan's new "chamber music" approach to Wagner, and many found the neo-Bayreuth production hardly worth the money that Eastern Airlines had invested in it or the publicity that had preceded it. In the *New York Times*, Harold C. Schonberg wrote:

> Act I was, to put it mildly, eccentric. Mr. Karajan seemed to work on the premise that if the voices are not big enough, the orchestra has to be cut down so that the singing can be heard. Following this premise, the conductor kept the dynamic level extraordinarily low, and the tempos rather slow. It was an ultra-refined chamber-music kind of sound that he drew from the orchestra . . . then for the rest of the opera Mr. Karajan suddenly presented a performance

that was much more conventional in tempo and dynamics . . . to traditionalists, the last two acts were much more convincing No Wagner conducting like it has been heard since the great old days. [*New York Times*, November 22, 1967]

Schonberg acknowledged that if one preferred the non-naturalistic approach to Wagner (and he didn't), then "it was hard to conceive of a production superior to last night." In an article a few weeks later, Schonberg made it very clear where he stood with respect to this sort of production. Zeroing in on designer Schneider-Siemssen's notes in the program book for *Die Walkuere*, Schonberg accused him, and by implication Karajan, of reading far too much into the *Ring*. The view which discovers parallels to the plight of modern man in the *Ring* he dismissed as "intellectual hogwash." But Wagner himself had been favorable to this sort of interpretation of his music dramas, and his grandson Wieland in recent years had redeveloped this approach at Bayreuth. Since myths like the *Nibelungenlied* are generally recognized today as a reflection of the social and psychological characteristics of many societies, it is rather odd that Schonberg should have been so harsh with this production. However, he was certainly not alone in his dismay over Karajan's conducting of Act I. In the *New Yorker*, Winthrop Sargeant was even more blunt:

Mr. von Karajan conducted a rather soft and unemphatic first act. Perhaps he was trying to underplay in order to achieve big climaxes later, but the effect was often muddy and the attacks were indistinct. Later on, he introduced some vigor, and things began to assume more virility. The kindest comment that one can make about his interpretation is that it is highly idiosyncratic. [*New Yorker*, December 2, 1967]

Thus, Karajan's debut at the Met and its latest production of the *Ring* were received with something less than universal admiration. Though many observers admitted that the Met orchestra hadn't played so well in years, they weren't able to reconcile themselves to the subdued atmosphere of the

79

first act and the absence throughout the performance of the bellowing one usually associates with the Wagner productions. Incipient *Heldentenor* Jon Vickers seemed to have lost his voice in his *Winterstuerme* in Act I, and Thomas Stewart as Wotan *spoke* rather than sang for much of Act II. Moreover, Gundula Janowitz' *Sieglinde* was positively Mozartian! To make matters worse, many couldn't understand why Hunding's dinner never appeared when he asked for it, or where he went when the stage directions indicate that he has gone into his house. In this symbolist production many of the familiar objects seemed to be ignored altogether. But as the weeks went by and reviewers returned for a second look, the new delicacy that Karajan brought to *Die Walkuere* began to seem less eccentric. After all, they recalled, Debussy greatly admired Wagner, and surely not for the orchestral tumult and superhuman singing. Perhaps, then, the customary desire for real Wagnerian singers is based on a mistaken idea of what the Wagnerian style is. Perhaps Wagner did not, after all, demand voices of heroic proportions but rather singers with modest voices who could interpret the text with intelligence, and conductors who were concerned not so much with the volume of the orchestral sound but with marrying the music to the words. Thus, the new Karajan approach could be viewed not as sheer perversity but as a return to Wagner's original conception. As for the stage production, it was clear that few in New York had been exposed to what Wieland Wagner had been doing for years in Bayreuth. And for all those who deplored the departures from naturalism, as many found that they could take Wagner's operas seriously for the first time. Much of what had formerly seemed silly when rendered naturalistically now became convincing when handled more abstractly.

Working closely with Karajan, Gunther Schneider-Siemssen designed an abstract and flexible basic set for the *Ring*, with an important role played by an elaborate pro-

80

jection system, much of which had to be purchased by the Met especially for this production. Furthermore, because the projection system was so new and so complicated, dozens of rehearsals were required for the lighting alone. Schneider-Siemssen explained his conception as follows:

> The *Ring* ellipse, which has a prominent position in all four works (in varying uses) has a visual, symbolical and technical function to fulfill. The unit is underscored by maximum use of new lighting and projection techniques. Through the use of this medium it is possible to dematerialize the stage and heighten the inherently dynamic qualities of dramatic action. In lighting every scene we have done away with the conventional "stationary lighting," which is an attribute of a static stage picture. Anyone who knows the score knows that the requirement is for "dynamic lighting," which must be many-faceted, forming a parallel to the musical leitmotifs. [*Metropolitan Opera Program*, Fall, 1967]

The impression one has from the Karajan-Schneider-Siemssen productions is of continuous and often imperceptible changes in lighting, which serve not merely to illuminate singers or objects but to relate the mood of the music as well. The technology now exists to do this, and Karajan and Schneider-Siemssen are among the first to show how well it can be used. By means of a series of hidden projectors and translucent screens, they have perhaps achieved the effect Wagner intended.

Birgit Nilsson, however, never got over the shock of singing her important role in nearly total darkness. Even when she showed up in a miner's helmet with a lantern attached, she failed to change Karajan's mind, and Nilsson has since taken her Bruennhilde elsewhere. Though still an admirer of Karajan's conducting, Nilsson is merciless about his abilities as a stage director:

> I still don't think he himself knows how wrong he is in his productions . . . when he makes all those light rehearsals, or dark rehearsals, he doesn't count on the fact that the orchestra pit is not lit. When the performance comes, he brings the pit up higher, you can see him from the knees up and he has a spotlight on him, of course.

81

The public gets all the light from the orchestra pit in their eyes. And the stage remains dark. It's insane; and nobody dares to tell him because they're afraid of him. This is the way Karajan feels he is great — that he has the power and nobody is worth anything around him. [*New York Times*, April 30, 1972]

Throughout the fall of 1967 Karajan dominated musical life in New York. Not only did he make his debut at the Met in a controversial new production; he also appeared at Carnegie Hall conducting the La Scala orchestra and chorus in the Verdi Requiem and later, for three evenings, conducted Bach with the Berlin Philharmonic. The Verdi was a memorable occasion (for those who could afford the inflated prices), but the Bach concerts again stirred the hackles of Winthrop Sargeant, among others:

Mr. von Karajan's duties seemed to be to wave a hand occasionally at the group, to plunk out the *continuo* at the second harpsichord, and to turn pages for Miss Bilgram. Otherwise, he was a mere ornament, though, to be sure, Mr. von Karajan is unquestionably ornamental . . . he might just as well have not been there as far as the musical result was concerned. [*New Yorker*, December 9, 1967]

The following season Karajan returned to the Met for another instalment of the *Ring* — this time *Das Rheingold* — and the critics fell over themselves showering praise on the production. Whether they had simply adjusted themselves to Karajan's Wagner interpretations or whether Karajan had actually been more successful with *Das Rheingold* than with *Die Walkuere* is not clear. In any case, Karajan's stock in New York had never been higher. In the *New York Times*, Harold C. Schonberg wrote:

. . . everything seems to work better in *Das Rheingold* . . . throughout the production, everything hung together, everything worked. There were style, mood, and the bigger-than-life feeling one is supposed to encounter in the *Ring*. [*New York Times*, November 23, 1968]

And Schonberg was echoed by David Hamilton in the *Nation*:

Herbert von Karajan's presentation of Wagner's *Das Rheingold* is a rather special event, offering a combination of musical and dramatic values only rarely present at the Metropolitan Opera — and, indeed, only partially present in Karajan's *Walkuere* of last season. [*Nation*, December 30, 1968]

At last Karajan's grandiose scheme for transporting productions from Salzburg to New York in order to attain the highest possible standards was vindicated. Recording the opera in December, performing it on stage at Salzburg the following April, performing it again in the fall in New York, each time with the same ensemble, provided a singularly imaginative solution to the economic difficulties that constantly threaten to undermine the standards of the modern opera house. Productions such as these point out the absurdity of performances, commonplace in New York, Vienna, and elsewhere, in which singers and conductors alike appear without any rehearsal whatsoever.

Unfortunately, no sooner had Karajan's scheme borne fruit than it ceased to exist. In the fall of 1969 the Met was hit by a series of strikes that forced the cancellation of half of its productions for the season. Due to the state of uncertainty that prevailed, many artists had to be released from their contracts, and the plans for Karajan's production of *Siegfried*, the third part of the *Ring* cycle, had to be scrapped. Since top-flight singers must often be booked years in advance, the cancellation played havoc with the entire Salzburg-New York scheme. *Siegfried* was produced at Salzburg in 1969 but could not be scheduled on such short notice for 1970; instead, *Die Goetterdaemmerung* was to be presented. After yearly postponements of the resumption of the *Ring*, Karajan and the Met went their separate ways and Karajan's involvement with the Met ended. The Salzburg-Met *Ring* has since been completed in New York but without Karajan as conductor. Admirers of *his* interpretations of Wagner will have to journey to Salzburg for the foreseeable future.

83

In the years 1955 to 1968 Karajan, as we have seen, was a frequent visitor to the United States, usually as head of a visiting ensemble from Berlin, Vienna or Milan. But after 1968 there was a hiatus of six years when Karajan did not return to the U.S. With his well-known dislike of guest conducting and the collapse of his *Ring* project at the Met, it is not surprising that he has not appeared with American ensembles in recent years. What is less understandable, perhaps, is his failure to reappear with visiting groups, especially the Berlin Philharmonic, in view of the current popularity of Karajan's recordings with them. The boxed set of the Beethoven symphonies is a perennial best-seller in the U.S., and various promotional gimmicks ("Hi-Fi Karajan" and "Karajan Express") have helped to remove the stigma of Deutsche Grammophon being too esoteric or foreign for the American market. Karajan and the Berlin Philharmonic also record now for EMI and Decca-London, thus enhancing their domestic marketability. In 1974 Karajan and the Berlin Philharmonic returned to the U.S. for a full-scale tour. It was a typical whirlwind affair: ten concerts in twelve days and appearances in only four cities, Washington, Boston, Chicago, and New York. The orchestra was presented by Columbia Artists and prices ranged as high as fifteen dollars. But apparently these concerts were loss-leaders. In New York, for example, to get into one Berlin Philharmonic concert one had to buy a series ticket that included recitals by two or three other performers. Subsequently it was announced at several of the concerts that the tour had been made possible "through personal and corporate funds." Most of the concerts were sold out far in advance.

The first concert of the tour took place in the new Kennedy Performing Arts Center in Washington. The program consisted of Beethoven's Fourth and Fifth Symphonies. Having heard Karajan do these works time and time again in previous American tours and in Salzburg, I wasn't expecting any revelations, and, as far as interpretation was concerned, there weren't any surprises. But what did astonish me was the sheer sound and intensity of the performance. It had been nearly two years since I had last heard a Karajan Berlin Philharmonic concert, and I had nearly forgotten just what that meant. The first point that ought to be mentioned is the seating of the orchestra, for that probably has a lot to do with the sound Karajan gets: strings at floor level with violins massed to the left, cellos in the middle, violas on the right, and basses spread out behind; winds on low risers, brass behind them on a higher level and, on the very top, the percussion. The timpani in the Beethoven symphonies were shattering, the brass no less so. But this is not to say that the balance was bad. In many orchestras the brass and timpani could only be that effective at the expense of the string choir. But the Berlin Philharmonic strings are too powerful for that. Even in the loudest and brassiest climaxes they are always "there." And what a dynamic range! In the Fifth the *pianissimo* from the basses and cellos at the beginning of the scherzo was unbelievable, whereas in the trio section their volume and intensity were hair-raising.

There are of course those who will say (and did say) that the Berlin orchestra is incomparable (doubtless due to Karajan) but that behind all the virtuosity there is nothing, for Karajan is simply interested in and obsessed with the manipulation of sound. But that was not my impression. I felt that this was the ultimate realization of what the composer had intended. Karajan is *not* invisible and if that's what people expect of a conductor then Karajan is not their man. To bring Beethoven's blazing vision to life in performance surely requires a force of personality no less blazing. And Karajan has a unique capacity for drawing from the hundred or so orchestra members everything they have in terms of both technique and feeling.

Karajan in his late sixties still has a youthful physical

presence; he is controlled in gesture and tightly coiled. One can actually see the climaxes coming as he gradually becomes more emphatic. He now conducts in a turtleneck sweater rather than in a boiled shirt — but for comfort rather than effect. At the Washington concerts there was another example of what many would take to be a typical Karajanism. After the intermission an announcement was made that the air conditioning was being turned off at Karajan's request (insistence?) because it was creating a draft. Karajan is apparently very sensitive to drafts. He has had many experiences of perspiring in rehearsals or performances, catching cold, and being laid up with back pains for days or even weeks after. But since Washington was than basking in a heat wave (temperatures were in the 80s) the effect of turning off the air conditioning was stifling.

From Washington the orchestra went to Chicago for two concerts. The highlight of the concerts was a performance of the Bruckner Eighth Symphony, which Karajan later described as "one of the ten best performances of anything I have ever given." In Boston where the orchestra appeared next, the instruments arrived only just in time for the concert and the players' dress suits failed to arrive altogether. There was no rehearsal and it showed. The Brahms Third Symphony, which opened the concert, was sloppy and nervous. But the Wagner *Tannhaeuser* Overture, which closed the program, was another matter. The Berlin Philharmonic had by then taken full measure of Boston's Symphony Hall and filled it with an awesome sound. The *Tannhaeuser* Overture is not one of my favourite pieces, and at one of the Washington concerts it did not become so even in Karajan's hands. But in Boston there seemed to be a new dimension to the music. In the words of *Christian Science Monitor* critic Louis Snyder there was an "epic majesty" in this performance, "a far cry from the chamber music approach that some have decried in Karajan's treatment of Wagner." And *Boston Globe* critic Richard Dyer

86

was even more impressed: "The sheer sound of it is so glorious that nothing much remains of the critical, even rational powers of anyone who listens."

But then in New York there was trouble once more for Karajan's detractors were out in full force. Harold C. Schonberg of the *Times* was favourable but reserved; Donal Henahan of the same paper was positively scathing:

> What a marvelous thing publicity is. Herbert von Karajan rides into town at the head of his Berlin Philharmonic, preceded by a thunderous thumping of drums and good sense flees before him . . . the Beethoven (Fourth Symphony) . . . far from representing a zenith for our time, was heartless, humourless and almost totally lacking in a sense of spontaneity. It was good machine-made music if you like that sort of thing . . . *A Hero's Life* was delivered by the conductor in an amazingly impersonal manner, like a brand-name product that everyone knows is good without opening the package. [*New York Times*, November 13, 1974]

And the *Musical America* critic, Stephanie von Buchan, shared his sentiments: "He ruined the Beethoven Fourth by offering a mannered, brutal reading that sounded as if it had been designed to get through to Beethoven a year after he went deaf." (*Musical America*, February, 1975) Obviously, Karajan and his performances still create controversy. To my mind, the Strauss performance described by Mr. Henahan as "amazingly impersonal" was nothing of the sort; well-prepared, certainly, but impersonal never! In fact, it was the most moving performance of the score I have ever heard. The exquisite tenderness of the violin and horn solos in the final pages was sublime. Perhaps Mr. Henahan, like so many others, is deceived by Karajan's physical movements for Karajan doesn't mirror the emotion of the music in extravagant gestures and facial expressions and therefore may appear to be somewhat detached. But he does communicate what he feels to his players and they certainly reflect this in their playing. In case Mr. Henahan hasn't noticed, the Berlin Philharmonic plays with more involvement than almost any other orchestra in the world.

87

They take extraordinary pride in what they do and with Karajan on the podium they play with an even greater commitment. As principal flautist James Galway put it: "Something happens when he comes on the platform that happens with no other conductor."

# 7
# The Karajan Empire

At one stage of his career Karajan was widely known as the *Generalmusikdirektor der Welt*, because of the fact that he held so many important posts simultaneously. He was director for life of the Berlin Philharmonic and the Vienna *Singverein*, he was director of the Salzburg Festival and the Vienna State Opera (and thereby chief conductor of the Vienna Philharmonic), and he was one of the chief conductors at La Scala. No other figure in the musical world held nearly as much power as Karajan during the period 1956 to 1964.

But all of these activities were interconnected, and all, except for tours with above-mentioned ensembles, were confined to continental Europe. Moreover, since 1955, Karajan has substantially reduced his world-wide activities as a conductor. Unlike most prominent conductors today he doesn't appear regularly with leading American orchestras in New York, Boston, Chicago, and so on; in fact, he never has. Though he has made frequent tours to various capitals of the world, most often they have been with the Berlin Philharmonic or with touring ensembles with which he is closely associated (as the 1959 world tour with the Vienna Philharmonic or the appearances in Moscow and Montreal with the La Scala Opera in 1967). Today Karajan rarely appears as a guest conductor. He has not guest conducted at all in North America since 1959 and has not appeared in England since 1960. He just does not see the point of such brief engagements when he can achieve much better results by working continuously with the same ensembles year after year in Berlin and Salzburg.

As recently as 1969 there was an important exception, which indicated that Karajan is still open to new challenges with orchestras other than the Berlin Philharmonic. At that time Karajan accepted an invitation to go to Paris, not as a guest conductor but as "musical counsellor" to the youngest and most prestigious of French orchestras. It has always been a source of amazement to foreigners (and of frustration to Frenchmen) that France has never had an orchestra comparable to the really great orchestras of Europe. Certainly there have always been fine French musicians — especially wind players — but never an ensemble to match the Berlin or Vienna Philharmonic or the Amsterdam Concertgebouw. With the creation of the new Orchestre de Paris in 1966 steps were finally taken to remedy the situation. Players from all over the world were auditioned by the musical director of the orchestra, Charles Munch, the greatest living French conductor. The orchestra's first concert was given in Paris in 1967. Apart from the quality of the players and the conductor, the principal advantages that the new orchestra acquired were a government subsidy and, as a result, a certain amount of security. Too often in the past French orchestras had to struggle desperately to make ends meet; and, with a steady flow of players to and from the orchestra, neither discipline nor quality could be maintained.

The new orchestra was soon in great demand all over the world and made an excellent impression wherever it played. Under Munch the orchestra enjoyed a spectacular triumph in Carnegie Hall during its first American tour. Unfortunately, however, later in the same tour, Munch died suddenly, and the continued development of the orchestra was thereby jeopardized. To safeguard the orchestra's international stature the French government sought out the most prestigious conductor it could find, for the orchestra had come to symbolize French culture itself, and its preservation was, therefore, of the utmost importance.

To nearly everyone's amazement, Herbert von Karajan was named to succeed the beloved Munch. In the past, Karajan had consistently refused such invitations on the grounds that his lifetime appointment with the Berlin Philharmonic made a relationship with another orchestra both unnecessary and impractical. It has been said by some, George Solti among others, that Karajan accepted the call from the orchestra because his wife was French and he thought it might be nice to have a French orchestra, too. But the fact is that Karajan had heard the orchestra under Munch at Carnegie Hall, and he had unbounded admiration for it. He made it quite clear, however, that because of his prior commitment to the Berlin Philharmonic, he could only accept the post of musical counsellor, and not of director. He further stipulated that he would continue to hold that post only, as he put it, until a suitable French conductor could be found. Under the agreement, Karajan was to spend only a few weeks each year with the orchestra, making recordings with it, and conducting its important engagements at festivals and tours abroad. Someone like Karajan was needed to lend prestige to the orchestra at a crucial moment in its development, and Karajan was only too glad to help. Unfortunately, this was not quite what the management of the orchestra had in mind, and they continually pressed Karajan to spend more time with the orchestra. Finally, the pressure became so great that Karajan was forced to resign, and the orchestra was dealt a serious blow.

Karajan's appointment to the Orchestre de Paris was a major event in French cultural life, as a lead article in *Le Figaro Littéraire* testified. When more than twenty leading

French musicians and critics were asked in the article, "Pour ou Contre Karajan", for an evaluation of Karajan's appointment, nearly all replied that Karajan was just what the orchestra needed.

Karajan conducted the orchestra for the first time in July 1969 for the festival at Aix-en-Provence. The major work on the program was Berlioz' *Symphonie Fantastique*, a work with which Munch had been closely identified. But the reaction to Karajan's more serious, less uninhibited interpretation of the work was very positive, and at its conclusion Karajan was applauded by both audience and orchestra members alike. According to the principal flautist of the orchestra, Michel Debost, while the Munch reading had been truly visionary, Karajan's interpretation had been equally fine in its own way.

Less than one year later, however, after a number of increasingly successful concerts together, Karajan resigned his post as musical counsellor of the orchestra. This was due to a number of circumstances. Karajan's initial contract ran from 1969 to October 1971. But whether or not he was to be granted an extension had to be determined in the spring of 1970, since artists had to be booked far in advance. When the contract was drawn up and a draft presented to Karajan, he indicated that it was acceptable to him. But when the final version of the contract was offered to him, Karajan discovered to his dismay that a number of terms had been altered, and altered in such a way that he could no longer accept the contract. Among the changes stipulated by the contract was that Karajan must accept the title of director of the orchestra, but Karajan had stated publicly on numerous occasions that he could never do so. This duplicity was apparently the work of Marcel Landowski, the government minister responsible for the orchestra. Without consulting the orchestra, he had decided, it seems, that Karajan's part-time involvement with the orchestra was not good enough. His judgement

92

may have been appropriate, but certainly the method he used to get rid of Karajan (to make way for George Solti) was not. Apparently, negotiations with Solti were secretly underway at the same time as Landowski was supposedly discussing the renewal of Karajan's contract. In a letter to Landowski, which was subsequently published in *Le Figaro Littéraire*, Karajan listed all the points that had been altered in his contract. His resignation hit Paris like a bombshell.

The orchestra itself sent a letter of protest to the minister, for Karajan and the orchestra had become very close, despite some trepidation that existed in the beginning that Karajan was merely a jet-setter. Karajan had proven himself in the short time that he was with the orchestra and once again the government had struck a blow for mediocrity.

Until the fall of 1971, Karajan continued to give concerts and to record with the orchestra but the American tour they had planned to make was cancelled. Subsequently, George Solti took over the orchestra, but within a short time he too was gone, for like Karajan, Solti had many appointments in many places and could not spend much more time with the Paris orchestra than Karajan could.

For Karajan the experience with the Orchestre de Paris taught him that it was no more possible to do justice to the demands of two orchestras than it would be to serve two wives. In the light of this experience he declined the offer to take over the Cleveland Orchestra after the death of George Szell and, for the foreseeable future at any rate, remains wedded to the Berlin Philharmonic.

One of the best recordings Karajan made with the Orchestre de Paris was the Franck Symphony in D Minor. This symphony, written in 1888, is now generally regarded as a curiosity from another age: it sounds too much like organ music; it stops and starts with annoying frequency; and its tunes are too self-consciously grand. But in Karajan's hands it becomes a masterpiece of beauty and meditation. The brooding quality he brings to the first movement foreshadows Sibelius, and the perfectly proportioned wood-wind chords reflect his incomparable ear for orchestral sonority.

Except for his brief and ultimately unsuccessful involvement with the Orchestre de Paris, Karajan has, in recent years, concentrated his attention on concerts with the Berlin Philharmonic and opera in Salzburg. But Karajan's activities today, while limited in view of the orchestras he conducts, are more breathless than ever before. While it may be misleading to call him the "musical director of the world," it certainly is no exaggeration to speak of a Karajan "empire."

First of all there are the films of opera and orchestral repertoire in which Karajan has become increasingly involved since 1960. It is difficult to say what motivates Karajan more: to bring *culture* to the masses or to bring *Karajan* to the masses. In any case, Karajan is steadily committing most of his repertoire to film in the same way that he has committed it to records. Karajan's approach is to record the music first; then film it later while the singers merely mime the roles. This enables Karajan to produce a work that is perfect both musically and visually. The films of *La Bohème, Carmen, Pagliacci*, and other operas are based on stage productions but are actually filmed in a studio. None of them, though, has really solved the most serious problems of putting opera on film — what to do during solo arias, how to capture the spectacle of an opera stage on a small screen, and so on — and few of them are ever shown on television. Most often they turn up in movie theatres, if they turn up at all. An unusual feature of most of the films is Karajan's Hitchcock-like predilection for appearing in bit parts: in a sombrero and a bushy mustache in *Carmen*; gesticulating from the audience in *Pagliacci* — very funny to Karajan's friends, no doubt, but more appropriate to home movies than to films with serious pretensions.

As for the· concert films, they, too, leave much to be

desired. In the Beethoven Ninth, for example, one sees little except violin bows, bells of trumpets, and the like, but above all, Karajan himself, eyes closed, making beautiful gestures. It's as if the members of the orchestra ceased to exist and the music was created by Karajan and a hundred instruments. One does not get the impression that the *players* expressed anything through the music — there is only Karajan. Truly an example of Karajan's narcissism in its most objectionable form. Yet, in other respects there is clearly an attempt to provide a viable visual counterpart to the musical substance, which is the fundamental problem of showing music on film. Karajan has sought to avoid shots of horn players emptying the saliva from their instruments or of players appearing inactive while performing. Though he has not solved the main problem — how to capture the sound of a full symphony orchestra in a visual medium — Karajan *is* one of the very few great conductors to interest himself in this problem.

One of Karajan's most recent projects involves the training of orchestral players, for most instrumentalists, according to Karajan, are encouraged to be soloists, and not enough attention is paid to training them for orchestral work. Because it is becoming increasingly difficult to get top players for the Berlin Philharmonic, Karajan is now offering scholarships whereby gifted young players study with members of the Berlin Philharmonic. The orchestra members are, in effect, training their own replacements, for the hope is that the scholarship holders will one day join the orchestra. But, of course, with such training these players could also join other orchestras if no immediate openings existed in the Berlin Philharmonic.

In addition, there are two Karajan foundations, one in Berlin and one in Salzburg. The Karajan *Stiftung* in Berlin holds yearly competitions, alternating between singers and conductors. Finnish conductor Okko Kamu won the first Karajan conducting competition and, as part of his prize,

95

recorded the Sibelius Second Symphony with the Berlin Philharmonic.

In Salzburg the Karajan Foundation is concerned with scientific research in such areas as the nature of musical experience, the value of music for psychotherapy, and so forth. Each year at the conclusion of the Easter Festival the Foundation presents a whole day of lectures and discussions in which Karajan himself takes an active part. The event is not well publicized and amounts to no less than a private seminar for Karajan.

All of these undertakings can be viewed both in a positive and negative light. In Karajan words, "Music has given me so much I want to give something back." But Karajan's critics see these activities as part of a grand scheme by Karajan to concentrate power in his own hands. At the very least, they will allow him to influence musical life for generations to come. And yet there is an obvious need for each of the enterprises in which he is involved. There is a shortage of good orchestral players, and there should be a way of preserving the tradition of the Berlin Philharmonic. After all, members of the Vienna Philharmonic are chosen in exactly the same way. New members are students of leading players in the orchestra. In this way there is some guarantee that the style of playing will remain constant. Similarly, there is a need for conducting competitions for, without them, there simply aren't enough opportunities for young conductors to establish themselves. Though such competitions do tend to favour quick study and superficial brilliance, they also open all kinds of doors for those bearing the Karajan imprimatur. As for the research undertaken by the Karajan *Stiftung*, it is too early to tell how much it will achieve, but it is at least admirable that a leading performer should take such an interest in some of the far-reaching implications of what he is doing. On one occasion Karajan even had himself wired with electrodes while conducting, so that his heartbeat could be measured.

96

In recent years Karajan's most ambitious project has been the exchange of opera productions between Salzburg, the Met, and any other opera house that is interested. Unfortunately, only the Met has shown a serious interest in the scheme, and only half the *Ring* cycle was produced there with Karajan in charge. But as recently as April 1973, at a press conference in Salzburg, Karajan was still promoting this type of international exchange on the grounds that there are not enough first-class singers around, that most productions are not rehearsed enough, and that costs are rising astronomically. Though all of these statements are perfectly true, it doesn't necessarily follow that Karajan's solution is the best one. In the first place, his idea would probably not result in a substantial saving. The Salzburg *Grosse Festspielhaus* is so much larger than any other in the world that sets cannot be transported from Salzburg to other opera houses. When the *Ring* went to the Met, the sets were built from scratch in New York. In addition, the Salzburg productions are based on a lighting and projection system that is practically unique, so that for the *Ring*, the Met was forced to invest heavily in new lighting equipment, even though it is among the most modern opera houses in the world. There is also the problem of unions. Unions in America will not allow productions to be mounted on their stages unless their own people are paid. If a Salzburg set is erected on the stage of the Metropolitan, the Met's scene builders are paid as if they had done the work themselves. Leading singers expect the same fee regardless of what opera house they sing in. Where, then, is the great saving?

Moreover, there is an argument for diversity. Is it really beneficial for one, and only one, *Ring* production to be seen at all the leading opera houses? As fine as Karajan's productions may be, there must also be room for productions by other leading artists. From the standpoint of quality and standards, however, Karajan's idea is perfectly reasonable. Most opera productions do suffer from too little rehearsal, and leading singers often jet from one house to another with no time for rehearsal at all. If, then, the singers and productions were moved together, this sort of problem could be avoided. For this reason, and perhaps this reason alone, Karajan's idea is worthy of adoption, at least on a limited scale.

In spite of the diversity of Karajan's activities and the obvious vanity and desire for power involved, Karajan has consistently resisted the temptation to compromise his standards. It is obvious, in fact, that the expansion of his power is very often an attempt to ensure those standards. Karajan could be guest conducting all over the world for enormous fees, in Los Angeles one day, New York the next, and so on. His name might be even more widely known than it is today. But he refuses to take this route and must be admired for so doing. Though one *can* criticize his extreme desire for power and control, his insistence on the highest standards does set an example that cannot be easily ignored.

# 8
# Karajan and the Critics

Karajan is certainly the best-paid and most influential
conductor of his generation. Perhaps because of this, his
detractors are many. Karajan's critics seem to fall into
three main categories: those who attack him on *political*
grounds; those who dislike him for *personal* reasons; and
those who find fault with his *musical* interpretations. The
first group includes those who protested against his first
appearances in the United States in 1955 and those indivi-
duals, such as members of the Jewish community, who, as
recently as 1967, objected to Karajan's possible appointment to the Chicago Symphony because of his former
membership in the Nazi party. In the eyes of such critics,
any consideration of Karajan's musicianship cannot be
divorced from moral or political issues. Many people object
to Karajan's *gauleiter* techniques. Members of the London
Philharmonia Orchestra, for example, were appalled by
Karajan's treatment of them and their audiences on a tour
of the United States in 1955. Others in this second group
of detractors point to the astronomical fees Karajan commands and the succession of tiffs he has had with management — especially in Vienna as director of the Opera. As
Martin Mayer put it:

On the whole he wants what he wants when he wants it . . . His reputation for outrageous demands is so strongly supported by history that quite sophisticated people a month ago accepted a preposterous story that his Met appearance might fall through because he had insisted on a "fresh orchestra" — men who had not played the night before — for his *Die Walkuere*. [*New York Times Magazine*, December 3, 1967]

Still others resent the kind of mystique that surrounds Karajan — from the fast cars and elegant women to the officious factotums and inspired arrogance of his platform manner.

In answer to some of these criticisms, Karajan's Nazi background did not seem particularly disturbing even to those Americans charged with denazifying him; in any case, the war has been over for nearly thirty years. As for Karajan's fees and his behaviour towards management, players, and audiences — for every individual who has been outraged, another has been charmed or convinced of the genuineness of Karajan's artistic integrity. Moreover, there are very few critics today who would rest their case against Karajan the musician on any of these grounds.

The most compelling criticisms of Karajan, then, are those that are based on (or at least purport to be based on) purely musical grounds, for these, in the final analysis, are the only ones worthy of serious consideration. But even in this category, Karajan's critics are by no means few in number or inconsequential; they include some of the foremost critics and musicians of our time. All have launched attacks on both live and recorded Karajan performances, and their reasons for doing so are often remarkably similar. To read critics such as Paul Henry Lang, William Mann, David Hamilton, and Martin Bookspan one would think that Karajan has risen to musical prominence solely on a combination of showmanship and business acumen rather than on the basis of musical ability. If one does take the trouble to analyze such critics' arguments, however, one is, I believe, impressed anew by the singularity and soundness of Karajan's aesthetic, for the arguments that so often are brought

100

to bear on his work reveal more in fact about the current assumptions and dogma regarding standards of musical performance than they do about Karajan.

Paul Henry Lang was Professor of Music at Columbia University and author of a number of books on music including the gigantic *Music in Western Civilization*, and formerly music critic of the *New York Herald Tribune*. He was also editor of the prestigious academic journal *Musical Quarterly*. Although Lang was enraptured by Karajan's New York concerts during the fifties, he devoted an unprecedented fifteen-page editorial in a 1964 issue of *Musical Quarterly* to a severe critical analysis of the Deutsche Grammophon recording of the complete Beethoven symphonies with Karajan and the Berlin Philharmonic. Throughout the article, Lang complains about the mediocre quality of the playing and conducting. Typical of the criticisms directed at Karajan are the following:

> In the *Eroica* . . . one begins to wonder, however, why this fine musician so often ignores one of Beethoven's most personal and powerful weapons, the *sforzando*. In a loud passage they are scarcely distinguishable from the ordinary *forte*.

> Perhaps the impression of slowness (in the slow movement of the *Pastoral* Symphony) is created by the rather monotonous articulation; the phrases do not rise and fall . . . The Seventh Symphony is pretty well played though the *portamentos* in the slow movement are rather surprising in view of Beethoven's dots over the notes. [*Musical Quarterly*, January, 1964]

Lang's criticisms are by no means atypical. Karajan is frequently taken to task, particularly in performances of Beethoven, for ignoring strong accents and for striving for smoothness of tone and texture above all else.

Similar comments about Karajan's recording of the Beethoven opera *Fidelio* were made by David Hamilton in the April 1972 issue of *High Fidelity*:

> The trouble with Karajan's approach is that it rides smoothshod over the structural aspect (there are, indeed, times when even the

simplest of accents, that which indicates the downbeat of the measure, is consistently suppressed) and yet it never brings forth much excitement either . . . Listen for accenting, the character of attacks and releases, the use of air space between notes and phrases, chord balances and clarity of voice-leading, variety and individuality of instrumental colors. I think you will end by agreeing that, as a performance of *Fidelio*, Karajan's is a pretty impoverished one, for all its surface "perfection."

Martin Bookspan has systematically refused to discuss Karajan recordings in his column "The Basic Repertoire" in *Stereo Review*. In response to a flood of letters from his readers asking why Karajan recordings were invariably ignored, he wrote:

I find Karajan's work antithetical to my tastes . . . I like sweep, passion, and chance-taking in my music, and respond coolly, if at all, to the taut, the controlled, and the precious . . . there is a quality of rigid calculation to much of Karajan's music-making that is downright offensive to my ears. [*Stereo Review*, January, 1970]

In *The Great Conductors*, Harold C. Schonberg reiterated the same general view of Karajan:

He proved to be one of the literalists . . . one who at his worst represented a sort of bored, dispassionate perfection . . . in recent years mannerisms have crept into Karajan's conducting: artificial-sounding tempos, unusual accents and emphases. [Victor Gollancz Ltd., London, 1968, pp. 324-326]

Though each of the critics cited thus far happens to be American, similar views have been expressed in European musical circles as well. William Mann, author of several books on Richard Strauss, chief music critic of the *Times* of London, and regular patron of Karajan's Salzburg Easter Festival, attempted to explain what he believed to be Karajan's principal defect as a conductor; Mann particularly took issue with the

. . . reverential and lifeless look at Mozart's *Requiem* by a master conductor and huge but effortful choir directed by Karajan at his most official and boring . . . These four Salzburg performances, including marvellous and deplorable readings, were united by a common interpretative menace: Karajan will not allow the music to breathe easily, he constantly shortens pauses and rests so as to jump ahead. [The *Times*, March 31, 1970]

This criticism dates from 1970; in 1972 Mann reacted to *Tristan* in much the same way: "I disliked Karajan's habit of racing over rests and holds so that the music's pulse got lost."

Mann's words have also been echoed by other English critics such as David Cairns:

Smoothness of line and tonal blend are the be-all and end-all. Even in the *Eroica* he ironed out the accents: there was not a true *sforzato* to be heard. Karajan's range of dynamics is surprisingly narrow. [*Responses*, Secker and Warburg, London, 1973, p. 166]

As we have seen, it is remarkable how much agreement there seems to be among leading critics concerning Karajan's performances. It is indeed difficult to recall other leading artists who have borne the brunt of so much criticism. And yet, there are precedents. Though Toscanini and Furtwaengler have now become legendary figures whose recorded performances enjoy widespread acclaim, they were not always so highly regarded. Many in the audience at Toscanini's concerts admired his precision but deplored his fast tempi and hard-driven approach; and countless musicians were dismayed by Furtwaengler's unpredictability and carelessness over matters of ensemble.

Despite the fact that only the most disparaging criticisms of Karajan have been presented, and the favourable, even adulatory comments that often appear in the same articles have been omitted, it is clearly not the case that Karajan is held in disfavour by most critics. Yet the implication is clear in many of the above remarks that the unfavourable judgements expressed are based on (or presumed to be based on) purely musical grounds and, as such, cannot be ignored by any serious musician. Even if the "facts" presented by the critics were substantiated, the judgements

103

based on these facts would not *necessarily* be negative. Furthermore, contained in such criticisms are a host of misconceptions and debatable assumptions pertaining to standards of musical performance, which oftentimes are not openly discussed. It is my belief that Karajan's approach, however much it can be criticized, is at least defensible on purely musical grounds.

In order to prove my point, I shall deal with the main criticisms of Karajan one by one and, by way of illustration, refer to the Karajan rehearsal records of Beethoven and Mozart, which have been published commercially. These recordings cast considerable light on Karajan's aesthetic, both theoretical and practical, and provide for its justification.

For the moment let us defer any discussion of criticisms based on value judgements or feelings, i.e., claims that Karajan performances are "wrong", "monotonous", "boring", "overrefined", and direct our attention to the *descriptions* by the critics of what, in their opinion, is taking place on record or in the concert hall. Since the line between objective description and subjective evaluation is often very thin, we shall, for the purposes of clarity, attempt to class the arguments against Karajan in one category or the other. Here are some typical criticisms.

(1) In his recording of the *Eroica*, Karajan ignores the *sforzando* marking. (Lang)
(2) In his recording of Beethoven's Seventh Symphony, Karajan ignores Beethoven's dots over the notes. (Lang)
(3) In his recording of *Fidelio*, Karajan suppresses accents, even those which indicate the downbeat of the measure. (Hamilton)
(4) Karajan shortens pauses and rests so as to jump ahead. (Mann)

Each of these criticisms claims that Karajan is doing something he *ought* not to do; ought, in most cases, because it represents a violation of what the composer actually wrote in the score. But, surprisingly, Harold C. Schonberg has categorized Karajan as "one of the literalists," and Hamilton

104

has written in the review of *Fidelio* from which we quoted earlier:

> Every note is played just as marked in the score, the players and singers are almost always in excellent ensemble, and the tempos are always reasonable interpretations of Beethoven's markings.

How is one to account for such apparent contradictions? The very same critics who contend that Karajan's interpretations are perverse claim that he scrupulously follows the composer's markings. How can it be said that Karajan plays exactly what Beethoven wrote, yet that he misrepresents Beethoven? The fact is that the critics in question are not really pointing out textual errors in Karajan's readings or describing what he does in any objective sense, since for the most part, they admit that Karajan does play what Beethoven wrote. What they take issue with (and they certainly are entitled to do so) is how Karajan *interprets* Beethoven. But instead of admitting that they are disputing interpretation, they give the impression that they are correcting obvious errors that any trained observer would recognize as errors.

In one sense, the critics are right: what actually happens on the recordings or in the performances under discussion does bear some relation to their description of what is happening, but in another sense, they are misdescribing what they hear. Thus, Karajan does not *ignore* Beethoven's *sforzando* markings, although his interpretation of them is not always as violent as, say, Toscanini's. Nor does he *ignore* Beethoven's dots over the notes in the slow movement of the Seventh, although his reading of them is different from Klemperer's or Szell's.

The key to understanding the whole business about *sforzandos* (and dots) lies in the recognition that a *sforzando* marking is not an *absolute* musical symbol as is

105

It is merely one of many musical symbols that must be interpreted according to the context. If I wrote *sfz* under the F written above, it would be impossible to render the sound without knowing the tempo and, probably, the context in which it occurred. I say probably because if such an indication occurred in a piece of contemporary music, the meaning would simply be *heavy accent*. But in Beethoven (the composer who concerns us at the moment), the *sforzando* is far more problematic. *Sforzando* means, literally, forcing. According to the authoritative *Harvard Dictionary of Music*, it is a sudden and strong accent on a single note or chord. But how strong? The *Harvard Dictionary* does not elaborate. That is up to the imagination of the interpreter. Since *sforzando* may be abbreviated as either *sf* or *sfz*, we shall use the one or the other, depending on the score that is being examined.

*Sfz* is a very rare marking in either Mozart or Haydn, but it is frequently encountered in the first movement of the *Eroica* and is very common in musical literature thereafter. What we must ask ourselves, then, is what it means and, more importantly, whether it means the same thing every time and in every musical context in which it occurs. My feeling is that *sfz* has many possible meanings, but always, of course, some kind of accent. In fact, I know of no recording or performance that has even attempted to render *sfz* in the same way throughout the first movement of the *Eroica*, the reason being that *sfz* cannot mean an explosive accent every time it occurs without distorting the melodic line beyond recognition. Furthermore, I cannot believe that this is how Beethoven meant it to be interpreted — however much this might suit our romanticized conception of Beethoven's personality — for the most cursory examination of Beethoven's scores reveals that accents are almost always indicated by *sfz* or its relative, *sfp*.

The fact is that an accent can be light or heavy, short or long, and will vary according to orchestration, phrasing, or

106

bowing. For example, the six *sf* chords which occur before E in the exposition of the first movement are *tutti* chords, very richly scored in the strings, suitable for successive downbows, and reinforced by timpani. They obviously can be very loud and very powerful, and are likely meant to be so. Whatever *sfz* means, this is probably the kind of context in which an explosive accent would be most appropriate. Contrast this use of *sfz*, however, with its use in the opening phrase of the movement, in the first violin. *Sf* on the A-flat in bar 10 still means accent, of course; but an accent comparable to the power of the *sfz* before E is neither possible nor intended. Here the *sfz* is used to indicate an accent at the apex of the melodic phrase, following a *crescendo* and preceding a *diminuendo*. The phrase itself is to be played *legato*, and the violins must make their accent on the first beat and continue playing the A-flat to the end of the bar and through two beats of the next, without changing bows. Since a heavy accent demands a lot of bow, the strength of the accent must be reduced enough to allow sufficient bow for the rest of the phrase. Almost invariably then, in performances of the *Eroica*, this *sfz* is not rendered as a heavy accent. Interpretative problems remain, however, regarding the precise character and duration of the accent. Should the violins give it a sharp jab or should they lean into it? There is often widespread agreement among musicians about such matters but, all too often, that agreement is based on nothing more than unquestioned habit, tradition, or unexamined dogma.

The point of our analysis is to determine the importance of discriminating between various interpretations of the marking *sfz*. Different orchestras naturally tend to interpret it in different ways and it is up to the conductor to decide whether the orchestra's interpretation coincides with his own. The conductor must also sort out the less obvious uses of *sfz* and the multitude of similar markings in an orchestral score.

In the *Eroica*, the passage from bars 23 to 35 features no less than twelve *sforzandos* and two *forte-pianos*. Conductor and orchestra must decide whether all the *sfz* deserve identical treatment or whether the logic of the phrase suggests that some be accorded greater weight than others. Here, again, bowing may be a consideration. The first violins cannot render the *sfz* in bars 25 and 26 as heavily as in bar 28 unless they play all downbows, and thereby break up the phrase and shorten the A. Listening to the solution effected by various conductors will reveal a good deal about both the *sforzando* in Beethoven and the relation of the conductor to the composer's markings. The conductor cannot simply read off the music mechanically, even if he wanted to. The notes on the page can only be transformed into sound when they have been interpreted. In any case, to say that Karajan *ignores* this or that marking in Beethoven, in the light of what is, in fact, a varied and subtle solution to a fundamental musical problem is unfair both to Beethoven and to Karajan and is, at best, the grossest misrepresentation of the conductor's responsibility.

The third criticism which Hamilton makes seems to raise a slightly different issue. To say that Karajan *suppresses* accents at the beginning of bars does not mean that he ignores one of Beethoven's markings, for there is no accent written over the notes in question. But, to Hamilton's way of thinking, it is somehow perverse or unmusical not to accent them. Certainly if one were *supposed* to accent such beats, Hamilton would be right; Karajan *does* suppress such accents. In fact, he is absolutely obsessed with avoiding what he would call "false" accents, as no one who listens to his rehearsal recordings of Beethoven and Mozart can fail to notice.

Listen to Karajan's interpretation of the opening melody of the Mozart G Minor Symphony. There are no accents on the strong beats (i.e., beats 1 and 3 in 4/4 time). Whereas most musicians tend to stress the first and third beats in

108

a 4/4 bar, especially when a melody contains the sort of figure we are dealing with here, Karajan tries to see the melody as a *whole*, without the bar lines, which, in any case, are merely a convenience for the performer and not a reliable guide for accent. (A comment by Karajan on this very point is included in Ernst Hauesserman's *Herbert von Karajan Biographie*, p. 88.) As a result, what we hear is not a motive that is repeated with accents on each D, but a melodic idea that extends to B-flat before there is a pause. This is especially important, since the melodic idea is itself part of a larger melodic unit. The smaller ideas lead to each of the succeeding ones, until all six or seven phrases are linked together to create an effect of unity throughout the first twenty bars of the symphony. Karajan achieves this unity, moreover, not simply by eliminating false accents, but by giving each note its proper value, particularly the repeated D and the final B-flat in the first phrase, and the final A in the second. But the tendency to clip these notes has very nearly become the rule among orchestral players today; Paul Henry Lang (who, as a musicologist, ought to be more circumspect about imposing absolute standards) even contends in a review of the Karajan recording that they *ought* to be played that way. What is more bizarre is his statement that Karajan's failure to do so reflects his failure to appreciate the importance of melody in Mozart. Karajan, of all conductors, surely gives Mozartian melody its due.

> Not every note of the opening theme should be *legato*; it makes a great difference if the third and sixth notes are not tied to the following ones. These are merely a couple of examples from among the many missed opportunities to phrase vocally.

For my part, I fail to see how such a rendering of the phrase in question is phrasing "vocally:"

**Allegro Molto**

Try to sing this passage with staccatos as indicated without producing a choppy, downright unmusical effect! The more natural and vocal reading is Karajan's:

**Allegro Molto**

The markings that I have added to the printed score simply indicate that these notes are to be given full value — that is, neither shortened nor accented. Karajan's reading of Mozart's melody follows all the markings of the original score and takes into account not only the idea itself but also the idea as part of a larger melodic unit.

The second and fourth criticisms of Karajan can be reduced to the claim that Karajan tends to ignore staccato markings (dots over the notes) so as to maintain continuity of line. It is true that Karajan takes a somewhat eccentric view of dots over notes. On the rehearsal record of the last movement of the Beethoven Ninth Symphony Karajan makes an illuminating comment as to how the following passage for violas and cellos should be played:

In the eighth bar of the passage there are staccato marks over each of the first two beats. (The metre here is 3/2.) When the orchestra plays the second beat short and naturally hesitates before the *pianissimo*, the result is an unwritten pause, which elicits the following dialogue:

*Karajan:* No, no! In time, in time! I want to go on until we reach the *pianissimo*! You always make an enormous pause which isn't shown — it's falsification of a document!

*Orchestra:* Yes, but what about the dots?

*Karajan:* They are only to get a good attack so that the notes are well articulated! They have nothing to do with the length of the notes; that's a fallacy, and let anyone who teaches it in an academy be turned out as a misleader of the people! In time!

111

The point here is that a staccato marking, like a *sfz* marking, is not an absolute but a relative symbol. Contrary to what pedantic music teachers impose on their students, a dot over a note is not to be interpreted as reducing the note to exactly half its value. If that were so, why not simply write in rests? Karajan overstates the case when he says that the dot has *nothing* to do with the length of the note. But it is true that while the dot indicates some shortening of the note over which it is written, the exact length is not indicated. In this particular passage, Karajan is surely right in saying that the dots have more to do with articulation or separation than with the length of the note.

The case of the slow movement of the Seventh Symphony is very similar, since it involves the interpretation of dots in slow tempo. While no commercial recording of Karajan's rehearsal for this passage is available, one can imagine that his remarks about it would have been very similar. Once more, I suspect, he would have contended that the dots tell the musician not to shorten the notes in question to half their value but simply to articulate or separate them. Shortening the notes too much produces an extremely choppy effect and tends to give the melody a trivial character rather than the sombre, somewhat doleful character that seems to have been intended. What Karajan aims for is accuracy, but accuracy does not mean literalism according to some kind of lexicon of musical absolutes. Instead, it means an accurate sound picture in terms of what the composer himself had in mind and sought to express by means of imperfect musical symbolism.

Too often the critics we have cited seem to misunderstand what musical performance is all about. The problem is not that Karajan has ignored or suppressed this or that in the score, but that his interpretation of the printed score differs from one which the critics have grown accustomed to or from one which, in their view, is more in keeping with the composer's intentions. If the latter is the case, (and it is surely the more charitable view to ascribe to them), then they must at least tell us why *their* interpretation of the composer's intentions is superior to Karajan's. As we have seen, the "facts" on which they base their criticisms are often not facts at all but subjective interpretations, and these require some justification.

Some critics might consider their interpretations preferable to Karajan's because, in their view, they are stylistically more correct. But style is a highly contentious matter too, and permits far greater flexibility than most critics would have us believe. Beyond certain superficial features, such as the *crescendos* and *pianissimos* indicated by the composer, Beethoven style or Mozart style depends as much on a conductor's imagination as on his musicological knowledge. While most musicians would agree, for example, that a stylistically correct performance of a Beethoven work must be based on an accurate rendering of all the notations indicated in the original score, there are, as we have tried to show, a number of possible interpretations.

Sometimes a composer is unaware of all of the possibilities his music holds, and it is not unusual for him to remark after a performance of his work by a gifted interpreter, "I had never thought of my music that way, but it certainly is interesting."

Toscanini, Furtwaengler, Walter, Kleiber and Klemperer — all have given us vastly different interpretations of Beethoven. Yet no critic could claim — much less prove — that their interpretations are stylistically *incorrect*. Similarly, Karajan's performances cannot be judged inacceptable on *factual* grounds. The critics must find a firmer basis for their arguments if they would have us accept their unfavourable judgements.

Turning then to the value judgements that have been made about Karajan, we may perhaps find them more plausible. But is it true to say that most people find Karajan's performances "unexciting", "overrefined", "boring", too "calculated" or "controlled"? Here the critics are offering not facts but feelings, and, while we might be persuaded to share their feelings, we are certainly under no obligation to do so. Reactions to a given piece of music vary notoriously from one listener to another. Many listeners find it extremely difficult to articulate how a piece has affected them for the simple reason that most music is very ambiguous, and the feelings it arouses in us are, likewise, ambiguous. In most cases, we must decide for ourselves whether or not we like a given piece of music. In forming our judgement, some knowledge of music would be useful, and the critics often help us to acquire that knowledge. But we must learn to distinguish between the *facts* they supply us and the *value judgements* often inherent in them, which do not necessarily follow. Specifically, as applied to Karajan, the "tight control" in his performances lamented by Bookspan and other critics and found by them to be ultimately boring, is considered by other observers, including myself, a source of extraordinary power, beauty, and excitement.

Karajan's critics, it seems to me, have failed to support their unfavourable judgements of his performances. As I have tried to show, their "facts" are often doubtful and contentious, and their opinions are based on no more than subjective impressions. While the critics no doubt, reflect current professional attitudes concerning musical performance, Karajan, in turn, reflects another philosophy, nurtured by a glorious tradition of musical performance in Berlin, Vienna, and Salzburg, and brought to fruition by more than forty years experience with the greatest orchestras and musicians of our time. It remains to be seen who will have the greater influence on musical practice in the future — the renowned practitioner or the respected theoreticians. But what is important is that the listener expose himself to Karajan's musicmaking with an open mind, and, more importantly, an attentive ear. If he does, I don't think he will be disappointed.

# 9
# Karajan's Influence

I have nothing against Karajan but if music would be as Karajan wants it, that would be the end of music. [composer-conductor Bruno Maderna in a *New York Times* interview, January 9, 1972]

In his late sixties, with the pattern of his life firmly established, Karajan is at the height of his powers and will likely continue his routine of fifty or sixty concerts a year with the Berlin Philharmonic and several operas a year at the Salzburg Festivals. Though his conducting style will probably remain essentially unchanged, as it has for many years now, his interpretations will no doubt deepen and mature, for Karajan is as ambitious as he ever was, as his recent interest in Mahler and the composers of the New Vienna School demonstrates. New direction in his life and art cannot be ruled out; yet an assessment of what has already been a full creative life is not altogether impossible at this time.

In an attempt to avoid obscuring Karajan's worth as an artist, very little has been said thus far about his personal life, which, like his life in the concert hall and opera house is dazzling and impressive. Karajan has always been extremely energetic — involved in a wide variety of sports activities from skiing to car racing — but he is also capable of extraordinary self-discipline, much of which he gained fairly late

115

in life, after his introduction to yoga. It is through yoga, perhaps, that Karajan learned to harness the nervous energy that at one time threatened to destroy him, for throughout his career one notes his tendency to collapse under duress. His new-found peace is probably also due in large part to his family life with his third wife, Eliette, and their two young daughters. Karajan is fulfilled both as a man and an artist, and the great wealth he has acquired in recent years has no doubt been a contributing factor. He is now able to maintain luxurious homes in Salzburg, St. Moritz, and St. Tropez, with indoor swimming pools, saunas, butlers and the like, and travels comfortably in a chauffered Rolls-Royce, accompanied by his personal bodyguard, an ex-policeman from Vienna. (Although as recently as 1971 he wrecked his souped-up Ford GT40 on a mountain road near Salzburg.) It is a glamorous picture one can paint of the Karajan lifestyle, but, in spite of fame and personal and financial security, Karajan remains extremely shy and ill-at-ease in his personal relations and goes to great lengths to be sheltered from press and public. A handsome man whose admirers are ecstatic in their praise of him, whose picture stares out of every shop window in Salzburg, who is renowned for the aesthetic beauty of his conducting style, whose every public appearance seems geared for maximum effect, Karajan, nonetheless, is a man in desperate need of solitude.

After a performance in Salzburg, Karajan and his wife are whisked away from the door of the *Festspielhaus* as king and queen, but Karajan goes home alone in the Rolls Royce, leaving his wife, who adores dancing and socializing, to attend the party at the *Goldener Hirsch*. Eliette von Karajan is the perfect mate and social director, playing the role of the surrogate and leaving Karajan free to concentrate on his art. A former French fashion model, Karajan's wife has never claimed to know much about music, and perhaps she doesn't, but she does serve a useful function in the Karajan organization, handling as she does Karajan's numerous social engagements.

Karajan also relies heavily on André von Mattoni to manage most of the day-to-day details of his professional life. As Karajan's personal secretary for several decades, manager of the Salzburg Easter Festival and, for all practical purposes, general manager of the Vienna State Opera during Karajan's directorship there, he occupies the most important post in Karajan's empire. He is in every respect the perfect choice for the role he plays: he knows Karajan's mind and conveys his wishes with charm and firmness; he is at least as meticulous and organized as Karajan himself; he is fluent in many languages; and his personal loyalty is beyond question. With Eliette to take care of his social life and Mattoni to manage his professional life, Karajan can well afford to be remote. There are, however some drawbacks to this system. Like too many presidents and political leaders, Karajan does run the risk of losing touch with his constituency and of being run by the machine he himself created. Rudolf Bing, for example, in his book *5000 Nights at the Opera*, complained that it was notoriously difficult even for him as General Manager of the Metropolitan Opera to communicate with Karajan personally. Moreover, by the time a message gets through the half dozen or so intermediaries employed by Karajan, it might be out of date. It is Birgit Nilsson who stated that among the people who work with Karajan, there is no one who would dare to criticize him.

Karajan *is* arrogant, vain, and prone to hide behind an efficient machine that runs his personal and professional affairs. But he is also a genius — perhaps the greatest conductor who ever lived — and it is the genuineness of his ability that does much to mitigate the less admirable features of his personal and corporate image.

First, that Karajan conducts hundreds of scores, including dozens of complete operas, from memory cannot be

117

considered merely as a gimmick. If it were, only one or two conductors in a generation could be said to have mastered this "gimmick." What this ability demonstrates is Karajan's intimate knowledge of the complexities of the scores he conducts, a knowledge that gives the singers and instrumentalists who play under him a sense of confidence, a standard to aim at, and an incentive to do their very best. When Lili Chookasian, in the midst of a recording of *Goetterdaemmerung* under Karajan, made one tiny mistake, singing two quarter notes instead of a dotted quarter and an eighth, Karajan (conducting without a score as usual) said nothing and merely waved his arm to indicate that they should stop and start again. On another occasion Jon Vickers went to see Karajan while he was preparing the role of *Tristan*, and asked him how he beat a particularly complicated passage in the third act. Though Karajan didn't have a score handy and hadn't conducted the opera for eleven years, he immediately was able to show Vickers how he did it.

In addition to being familiar with the notations of the written score, it is imperative that the conductor have a considerable knowledge of the style and sense of the music. Karajan has this to a greater extent than do most other conductors. In Wagner and Bruckner his breadth of line, range of dynamics and expression are unequalled. In any large-scale symphonic work, whether Beethoven or Shostakovich, his sense of structure and tension is truly astounding. While it may be true that Karajan's Stravinsky is nearly always too smooth where it should be spiky, that his Mozart for the same reason is often unsatisfying, that his performances of the great sacred choral works can sometimes be, to use William Mann's phrase, "reverential and lifeless," inherent in all he does is an intensity of concentration and a thoroughness of preparation. There is no such thing as a slapdash Karajan performance. With certain limitations Karajan commands a wide-ranging repertoire in which he excels to an extent rivalled by few other conductors who ever

118

mounted a podium. Toscanini was a master of Beethoven, Brahms, Italian and German opera; Karajan encompasses all these, but much more besides, including Bruckner, Mahler, Berlioz, and Strauss opera. As for Furtwaengler, in comparison with Karajan his experience in the opera house was practically non-existent, and his interest in contemporary music was at best perfunctory.

It is Martin Bookspan who said, with no compliment intended, that records mirror the man, and that Karajan the conductor, is perfectly represented by what one hears on his recordings. I do not share Bookspan's dismissal of nearly everything Karajan ever did, nor do I accept the view that Karajan's art is faithfully represented by his records. While Karajan is perhaps the first great conductor to commit his whole repertoire to recordings that in any way approximate the actual sound of an orchestra in a concert hall, and many of his records are superb documents of what he can do (much of the *Ring* cycle, the Tchaikovsky symphonies as recorded by EMI, the Rachmaninoff Second Piano Concerto with Weissenberg, the Schumann Second Symphony for Deutsche Grammophon), seldom if ever has the magic of a Karajan live performance been captured on a recording. The tapes from the Salzburg Festival of *Tristan*, *Die Goetterdaemmerung*, and *Boris Godonov* make Karajan's commercial studio recordings of the same period seem pale and unreal by comparison; even these tapes of actual performances are inadequate for the simple reason that they fail to convey the *visual* dimension of a Karajan performance — one of its most vital ingredients. By "visual dimension," we are not referring to the playing or conducting of an orchestra, for these cannot be construed as *acting* in any conventional sense. Nor are we referring to the miming and calisthenics in which some conductors indulge, for Karajan does not make faces to mirror the emotion of the music and he certainly does not dance or leap in the air à la Bernstein. Karajan's visual complement to the music is, therefore,

119

of a more abstract nature, more akin perhaps to the movements of a ballet dancer, though, in Karajan's case, the movement is confined to the arms and upper part of the body.

Many observers, such as music critic Jean d'Udine, consider dancing the bodily expression of the movement inherent in music. In the words of this critic, "The expressive gesticulation of an orchestra conductor is simply a dance." It is then altogether reasonable to view Karajan's movements as a conductor in this light. And, by so doing, one begins to understand why Karajan holds audiences spellbound. Like a great ballet dancer he provides them with a series of gestures that express the nature of the music he is conducting and makes clearer to them (and to the players, too, as they will readily admit) music that would otherwise be exceedingly difficult to make sense of in purely musical terms. In one sense of course, every conductor makes the music clearer to the orchestra through movement. But not every conductor makes the *meaning* of the music clearer, for not every conductor is a Karajan. Karajan does not give cues for the players to begin playing or to stop playing, nor does he indicate the bar lines with the usual up-and-down movement. These conductorial gestures may be necessary for the security of most performers, but are superfluous when a piece has been prepared in rehearsal as completely as a Berlin Philharmonic performance under Karajan.

The most important aspect of conducting *qua* dance as practised by Karajan (and, to a lesser degree, by some other conductors) is that the movements or gestures are not intended as *self*-expression. It is not *himself* that Karajan is expressing in gesture, but the music. Again, this is analagous to dance insofar as the movements and gestures of a dancer can only superficially be considered as self-expression; properly perceived they are part of a logic of expression in the same way that the lines spoken by an actor reflect not his feelings but the feelings of the character he is playing

120

and relate to the play as a whole rather than to the artist's own life. It is certainly easy to misinterpret Karajan's gestures and think that Karajan is expressing *himself*, because many conductors do just that. But to imagine that this is what Karajan is doing would lead one to the conclusion that he has no feelings, that he is oblivious to the sadness or turmoil of the music. And the countless critics who have charged Karajan with such coldness or insensitivity have obviously failed to understand what he is doing.

Because of Karajan's manner of conducting, in a large work such as a Bruckner symphony the attention of the audience is not continually drawn to the bits and pieces — a clarinet entry here, a horn solo there. The audience is not continually forced to concentrate on the mechanics of the performance, that is, the conductor's attempts to keep the players together, to make them enter and exit at the right places, to make them play this loud or that soft. Nearly all of these details have been taken care of in rehearsal. This leaves the conductor free to convey to his players the logic of the *whole symphony*. Similarly, he conveys the same information to the audience. A Bruckner symphony is not about instruments entering and exiting; it is about blocks of sound, variously organized, and it is the logic of this organization that Karajan communicates through gestures.

No one can deny the extraordinary impact that Karajan makes on the audience. Over and above his purely musical abilities, Karajan has an amazing capacity to inspire the orchestra to give its very best as well as to produce in the audience "a willing suspension of disbelief." It is this theatrical quality that helps to make Karajan a superstar; but it also makes him fair game for those who think conductors ought to be less concerned with effect.

To what extent has Karajan influenced the contemporary music scene? Nearly every young conductor these days seems more or less modelled on Karajan. Nearly all make a point of conducting without a score. Zubin Mehta, Seiji

121

Ozawa, Claudio Abbado all show the influence of Karajan, though each is a major talent in his own right. But whether these conductors will emerge as Karajans themselves remains to be seen. What they lack most of all is Karajan's vast experience (particularly opera). Unlike Karajan each made his mark in the concert hall before being invited to make a debut in a major opera house; in each case the result was disastrous. Each is in great demand today because music is like any other business: whoever draws a crowd is successful, and the conductor with charisma, with an image, wins out over his less glamourous, if sometimes more musical, colleagues. Though Karajan has long since proven that he is much more than a glamourous figure, he was among the first to show the commercial potential of star qualities in the world of classical music. Whether or not this will eventually be detrimental to music remains to be seen. Certainly the view expressed (at the head of this chapter) by the late Bruno Maderna and shared by Hans Werner Henze and many other composers is worth taking seriously. The star conductor often gets in the way of the music. For him, the music only seems to exist as a kind of raw material for his self-glorification. And Karajan *is* a star conductor *par excellence*. His box-office power has been almost unparalleled for years all over the world. And his power is such that he has been able to have his own way with a large number of major musical institutions. His influence has stretched even further. The singers he chose for the Vienna State Opera often became stars elsewhere simply on the basis of their association with him. In terms of repertoire, soloists, and guest conductors he has made his mark on concert and opera life in Berlin, Salzburg, Vienna, and far beyond.

There is no doubt that Karajan has this power. The question is how it has been used. No one denies that Karajan has encouraged, perhaps even discovered and nurtured, a large number of performers. But many would say that he has

122

done far less for composers. The reason he is singled out, of course, is that he has been in a unique position. He has had sufficient stature to play whatever piece he wanted to play. He has been in a position to use his unique power and talent as he wished. But what galls some of his contemporaries is that he chose to use his influence and prestige in other ways, apart from the championing of avant-garde music. Above all, he chose to seek standards of performance in the existing repertoire beyond what generally passed for acceptable. He chose to work with a single orchestra, for the most part, and to break out of the shoddy and frustrating routine of even the best opera houses. He also chose to take advantage of the latest technology to make the staging of opera a new and creative adventure, and to experiment with music on film so as to reach a much wider audience.

Hans Werner Henze found Karajan an ideal interpreter of his music: Karajan's performance of his Sonata for Strings was stunning. But what is so frustrating for Henze is that Karajan plays so little of his music or the music of any other living composer. Karajan has both the presitge and the talent to be of immense help to contemporary composers but chooses to direct his attention elsewhere. Perhaps only time will tell whether Karajan's energies were misdirected.

Whatever one may think of the way in which he applies his immense talents, Karajan *is*, nonetheless, a great conductor. It is my hope, therefore, that he will be remembered for the high standards of performance he has set and for the great interpretative insight he has brought to a vast repertoire, rather than for the controversial conductorial image he has helped to create.

# Discography

Generally speaking, Karajan's recording career falls into five parts: (1) up to 1945, a few recordings with the Berlin Philharmonic, the Berlin State Opera Orchestra and the Concertgebouw Orchestra; (2) recordings between 1946 and 1950 with the Vienna Philharmonic; (3) recordings made between 1948 and 1960 with the Philharmonia for English Columbia/Angel; (4) recordings made in the late 1950's and early 1960's with the Vienna Philharmonic for English Decca/London; (5) recordings made since about 1960 with the Berlin Philharmonic for Deutsche Grammophon. Since 1969, Karajan has recorded mostly with the Berlin Philharmonic for three labels: DG, EMI/Angel and Decca/London. The recording date, where known to us, is in brackets. It represents the day of the final recording session.

Performing as soloists in these recordings are the following artists:

**BASSOON**

Manfred Braun    Cecil James    Guenter Piesk

**CELLO**

Ottomar Borwitzky    Pierre Fournier    Msitislav Rostropovich

**CLARINET**

Karl Leister    Herbert Staehr    Bernard Walton

125

## FLUTE
Andreas Blau   James Galway   Matthias Ruetters
Karl-Heinz Zoeller

## HARP
Fritz Helmis

## HARPSICHORD
Edith Picht-Axenfeld

## HORN
Dennis Brain   Alan Civil   Norbert Hauptmann   Shirley Hopkins
Gerd Seifert

## OBOE
Karl Steins   Lothar Koch   Sidney Sutcliffe

## ORGAN
Anton Heiller   Wolfgang Meyer   Josef Nebois   Rudolf Scholz
Dennis Brain

## PIANO
Géza Anda   Lazar Berman   Shura Cherkassky   Walter Gieseking
Kurt Leimer   Dinu Lipatti   Hans Richter-Hasser   Sviatoslav
Richter   Alexis Weissenberg

## TRUMPET
Maurice André   Adolf Sherbaum

## VIOLIN
Thomas Brandis   Christian Ferras   Gidon Kremer   David
Oistrakh   Michel Schwalbé

## SINGERS
| | | |
|---|---|---|
| Theo Adam | Teresa Berganza | Helge Brilioth |
| Cvetka Ahlin | Carlo Bergonzi | Lilo Brockhaus |
| Maria Garcia Allegri | Walter Berry | Sesto Bruscantini |
| Luigi Alva | Maurice Besancon | Eberhard Buechner |
| Sylvia Anderson | Franz Bierbach | Maria Callas |
| Helja Angervo | Peter Bindszus | Enrico Campi |
| Wolfgang Anheisser | Jussi Bjoerling | Mario Carlin |
| Libero Arbace | Sigurd Bjoerling | Joan Carlyle |
| Agnes Baltsa | Franz Boeheim | Boris Carmeli |
| Fedora Barbieri | Mario Borriello | Carlo Cava |
| Ettore Bastianini | Kaja Borris | Athos Cesarini |
| Ugo Benelli | Aldo Bottion | Lili Chookasian |
| Jean-Christophe Benoît | Heinz Borst | Rudolf Christ |
| Hans Berg | Rolf Boysen | Plinio Clabassi |

126

Franco Corelli
Fiorenza Cossotto
Carlo Cossutta
Regine Crespin
Hugues Cuenod
Biserka Cvejic
Hilde Czeska
Friedrich Dalberg
José van Dam
Lucia Danieli
Bernard Demigny
Anton Dermota
Helga Dernesch
Anton Diakov
Najejda Dobrianowa
Oralia Dominguez
Helen Donath
Karl Doench
Eleonore Dorpinghans
Otto Edelmann
Renato Ercolini
Barbro Ericson
Geraint Evans
B. Fasolt
Werner Faulhaber
Anny Felbermayer
Wilhelm Felden
Dietrich Fischer-Dieskau
Mirella Freni
Siegfried Rudolf Frese
Brunnhild Friedland
Karl Friedrich
Catherine Gayer
Nicolai Ghiaurov
Erik Geisen
Mechthild Gessendorf
Peter Glossop
Tito Gobbi
Omar Godknow
Josef Greindl
Kay Griffel
Donald Grobe
Elke Grosshans
Elizabeth Gruemmer
Hilde Gueden
Giangiacomo Guelfi
Ernst Haefliger

Elizabeth Harwood
Martha Heigl
Hans Helm
Leo Heppe
Ruth Hesse
Horst Hiestermann
Marga Hoeffgen
Grace Hoffman
Werner Hollweg
Elizabeth Hoengen
Hans Hopf
Hans Hotter
Evamaria Hurdes
Maria von Ilosvay
Josef Janko
Gundula Janowitz
Helga Jenckel
Hannes Jokel
Sena Jurinac
Paul Karolidis
Zoltan Kélémen
Robert Kerns
Gwendolyn Killebrew
Peter Klein
Waldemar Kmentt
René Kollo
Erika Koeth
Otakar Kraus
Tom Krause
Helmut Krebs
Werner Krenn
Ernst Krukowski
Paul Kuen
Erich Kunz
Horst R. Laubenthal
Eleanor Lausch
Catarina Ligendza
Margarita Lilowa
Monique Linval
Wilma Lipp
George London
Emmy Loose
Colette Lorand
Glenys Loulis
Kari Loevaas
Christa Ludwig
Horst Lunow

Genevieve Macaux
Mario Machi
Cornell MacNeil
Gianni Maffeo
Erich Majkut
Stefania Malagù
Ira Malaniuk
Simone Mangelsdorff
Daniza Mastilovic
Sabin Markov
Jane Marsh
Luise Martini
Alfredo Mariotti
Adriane Martino
Aleksei Maslennikov
Edith Mathis
André von Mattoni
Giulio Mauri
Robert Merrill
Nan Merriman
Josef Metternich
Kerstin Meyer
Karl Mikorey
Olivera Miljakovic
Arnold van Mill
Anna Moffo
Kurt Moll
Mario del Monaco
Leonardo Monreale
Guiseppe Morresi
Edda Moser
Erna Maria Muhlberger
Alfred Neugebauer
Birgit Nilsson
Fritz Ollendorf
Carlotta Ordassy
Catherine Ott
Lisa Otto
Piero de Palma
Hermann Patzalt
Rolando Panerai
Milen Paunov
Luciano Pavarotti
Heinrich Pflanzl
Gernot Pietsch
Herman Christian Polster
Zvonimir Prelcec

127

Herman Prey
Leontyne Price
Carol Prichett
Harald Proglhof
Aldo Protti
Gregor Radev
Eugenia Ratti
Liselotte Rebmann
Heinz Reeh
Heinz Rehfuss
Maria Theresa Reinoso
Karl Renar
Regina Resnik
Anna Reynolds
France Ricciardi
Karl Ridderbusch
Friedl Rieger
Marius Rintzler
Manfred Roehrl
Hilde Roessel-Majdan
Nello Romanato
Hans Joachim Rotzsch
Marjan Rus
Leonie Rysanek
Ana Raquel Satre
Elke Schary
Wolfgang Schieder

Rudolf Schock
Peter Schreier
Hedwig Schubert
Else Schuerhoff
Rosl Schwaiger
Elizabeth Schwarzkopf
Irmgard Seefried
Michel Sénéchal
Frank Schooten
Ruth Siewert
Leopold Simoneau
Giulietta Simionato
Tomaso Spartora
Ludovico Spiess
Guiseppe di Stefano
Ingrid Steger
Hermine Steinmassl
Giorgio Stendora
Thomas Stewart
Teresa Stich-Randall
Gerhard Stolze
Teresa Stratas
Erich Strauss
Rita Streich
Annelies Stueckl
Joan Sutherland
Guiseppe Taddei

Martti Talvela
Heinz Tandler
Renata Tebaldi
Lieselotte Thomamuller
Jess Thomas
Anna Tomowa-Sintow
Herta Toepper
Gerhard Unger
Peter Ustinov
Astrid Varnay
Martin Varnay
Josephine Veasey
Jon Vickers
Luisa Villa
Galina Vischnevskaya
Siegfried Vogel
Eberhard Waechter
Ludwig Weber
Hans Wegmann
Bernd Weikl
Herbert Weiss
Ljuba Welitsch
Elfriede Wild
Erwin Wohlfahrt
Fritz Wunderlich
Nicola Zaccaria
Giuseppe Zampieri

## CHORUS MASTERS
Norbert Balatsch
Roberto Benaglio
Helmut Froschauer
Uwe Gronostay
Walter Hagen-Groll

Norberto Mola
Horst Neumann
Wilhelm Pitz
Herbert Schernus
Reinhold Schmid
Gerhard Schmidt-Gaden

## VOCAL COACH
August Everding

## CHOIRS (preceded by abbreviations used in these listings)

|  | Bancrofts School |
| --- | --- |
| BFC | Bayreuth Festival Chorus, 1951 |
| DOC | Chorus of the Deutsche Oper, Berlin |
| CRC | Cologne Radio Choir |
| DSOC | Dresden State Opera Chorus |
| LSMC | La Scala, Milan Chorus |
| LRC | Leipzig Radio Chorus |
|  | Loughton High School for Girls |

| PC | Philharmonia Chorus |
| RIASK | RIAS Kammerchor |
| SRC | Sofia Radio Chorus |
| TK | Toelzer Knabenchor |
| VBC | Vienna Boys Choir |
| VGKC | Vienna Grosstadtkinderchor |
| VSOC | Vienna State Opera Chorus |
| VS | Singverein der Gesellschaft der Musikfreunde, Wien |

**ORCHESTRAS** (preceded by abbreviations used in these listings)

| BFO | Bayreuth Festival, 1951 |
| BPO | Berlin Philharmonic |
| BSOO | Berlin State Opera |
| BSKO | Berlin Staatskapelle |
| CRSO | Cologne Radio Symphony |
| COA | Concertgebouw, Amsterdam |
| DSO | Dresden State Orchestra |
| LSMO | La Scala, Milan |
| LFO | Lucerne Festival Orchestra, 1950 |
| OdP | Orchestre de Paris |
| PO | Philharmonia, London |
| RIASO | RIAS Symphony |
| EIARSO | Italian Radio, Turin |
| VPO | Vienna Philharmonic |
| VSOO | Vienna State Opera |
| VSO | Vienna Symphony |

All known commercially released Karajan recordings are listed in this discography. North American, British and some German numbers are given. Performances are listed chronologically. Catalogue numbers shown are usually for the original issue. Because of repackaging and re-coupling, numbers can change. Check current catalogues for availability. Mono records are in *italics*.

## KEY TO RECORD IDENTIFICATION

**MONO**

| L, LB, LV, LVX, LX, GQX | EMI | 78 rpm |
| PD | Polydor | 78 rpm |
| 33C | English Columbia 10"LP | |
| 33CX | English Columbia 12"LP | |
| AL | North American Columbia 10"LP | |
| ML, RL | North American Columbia 12"LP | |
| SL, EL | Multiple sets of ML and RL | |

| | |
|---|---|
| DL | North American Decca LP |
| LE | Limited Edition USA |
| TC | Top Classic (Germany) |
| 6030 E | Seraphim 5 record set.<br>Angel Mono's are italicised. |

## 12″STEREO

| | |
|---|---|
| ASD, SEOM, ST, SAX | EMI |
| SLS, SMS | EMI Boxed Sets |
| SM | EMI pseudo stereo |
| SME | German EMI pseudo stereo |
| 5BB, SXL, SET, SDD, SPA | English Decca |
| CS, OS, STS | London |
| OSA | London Boxed OS's |
| LDS | RCA |
| 35000, 36000, 37000 | Angel |
| 3500, 3600, 3700 | Angel Boxed Sets. |
| B=2, C=3, D=4, etc. | suffix indicates number of discs. |
| 109 000, 135 000, 136 000,<br>139 000, 643 000,<br>2530 000, 2563 000 | Deutsche Grammophon |
| 2707 000 | DG 2 record Set |
| 2709 000 | 3 record Set |
| 2711 000 | 4 record Set |
| 2713 000 | 5 record Set |
| 2716 000 | 6 record Set |
| 2720 000, 2740 000 | indicated by number in brackets. |

## QUAD

Starting at about 37000 Angels are SQ encoded and can be identified by the circular Angel logo on the front of the album. EMI were issuing some SQ albums in addition to stereo, but after September 1975 only compatible quad/stereo have been issued. DG and Decca/London have issued none at this time.

## TAPES

Many tapes have been issued in reel-to-reel format. Decca/London and DG recordings are available for the moment from Ampex but will be discontinued by mid-76. Consult current catalogues for cassettes and 8-tracks.

# ADAM
Giselle – Suite      VPO CS 6251      SXL 6002 (9/61)

# ALBINONI
Adagio in G Minor for Strings
and Organ
Meyer      BPO 2530 247

# BACH J.S.
Brandenburg Concertos
– complete
   No. 1 Schwalbé,
   Steins, Civil, Hopkins
   No. 2 Scherbaum,
   Zoeller, Koch,
   Schwalbé
   No. 3
   No. 4 Schwalbé,
   Zoeller, Ruetters
   No. 5 Zoeller,
   Schwalbé, Picht-
   Axenfeld
   No. 6
Orchestral Suites
   No. 2 Zoeller
   No. 3      BPO 2709 016
Mass in B Minor
   Schwarzkopf,
   Hoeffgen, Gedda,
   Rehfuss, VS      PO *3500 C*      *33 CX 1121-3*(30/11/52)
   Janowitz, Ludwig,
   Schreier, Kerns,
   Ridderbusch, VS,
   Froschauer      BPO 2740 112      (3)

St. Matthew Passion
   Janowitz, Ludwig,
   Schreier, Laubenthal,
   Berry, Fischer-Dieskau
   Diakov, VS, Hagen-
   Groll      BPO 2711 112

# BALAKIREV
Symphony in C Major  PO *33 CX 1002*      (21/11/49)

# BARTOK
Concerto for Orchestra PO *35003*      *33 CX 1054* (22/7/53)
                       BPO 139 003
                       BPO 37059      ASD 3046 (30/5/74)

Music for Strings,
Percussion and Celesta   PO *ML 4456*
                         BPO 35949              SAX 2432 (11/11/60)
                         BPO 2530 065

**BEETHOVEN**
Fidelio – complete
  Vickers, Dernesch,
  Ridderbusch,
  Laubenthal, Donath,
  Kélémen, van Dam,
  Hollweg, Frese,
  DOC, Hagen-Groll    BPO 3773 C             SLS 954 (12/70)
Overture              BPO 139 001
                      BPO SEOM 18            (12/70)
Abscheulicher
  Schwarzkopf         PO *35231*             *33 CX 1266* (10/11/54)
Missa Solemnis
  Schwarzkopf,
  Ludwig, Gedda
  Zaccaria, VS,
  Schmid              PO 3595 C              *33 CX 1634-5* (16/9/58)
  Janowitz, Ludwig,
  Wunderlich, Berry,
  VS, Schmid,
  Schwalbé, Nebois    BPO 2707 030
  Janowitz, Baltsa,
  Schreier, van Dam,
  VS, Froschauer,
  Scholz, Brandis     BPO 3821 B             SLS 979 (28/9/74)
Egmont – Incidental
Music
  Janowitz            BPO 2530 301
Grosse Fuge           BPO 2530 066
Symphonies
complete              PO SM 143-9
                      BPO 2720 007           (8)
No. 1 + Overtures: Egmont, Leonore 3
                      PO *35097*             *33 CX 1136* (21/11/53)
                                                          (15/7/53)
No. 1                 BPO 138 801                         (14/7/53)
No. 2 + Coriolan Overture
                      PO *35196*             *33 CX 1136* (23/11/53)
                                                          (15/7/53)
No. 2                 BPO 138 801
No. 3                 PO *35000*             *33 CX 1046* (22/11/52)
                      BPO 138 802

132

No. 4 + Ah Perfido
   Schwarzkopf        PO *35203*           *33 CX 1278* (19/11/53)
                                              (20/11/54)
No. 4               BPO 138 803
No. 5               VPO *RL 3068*     *33 CX 1004* (17/11/48)
                     PO   *35231*       *33 CX 1266*
                     BPO 138 804
No. 6               PO   *35080*       *33 CX 1124* (10/7/53)
                     BPO 138 805
No. 7               BSKO *PD 68006-10*
                     PO   *35005*   ·    *33 CX 1035* (30/11/51)
                     VPO STS 15107    SDD 232 (3/59)
                     BPO 138 806
No. 8               VPO *EL 51*       *LX 988-90*
                     PO   *35301*       *33 CX 1392* (20/5/55)
                     BPO 138 808
No. 9
Schwarzkopf, Hoengen, Hotter,
   Patzak, VS        VPO *EL 51*       *LX 1097-1105*
   Schwarzkopf,
   Hoeffgen, Haefliger,
   Edelmann, VS     PO   *3544B*      *33 CX 1391-2* (29/7/55)
   Janowitz, Roessel-Majdan,
   Kmentt, Berry, VS,
   Schmid            BPO 2707 013
Rehearsals for 2707 013
   Movements 1 & 2   BPO 109 106
         4 only   BPO 643 201
Wellington's Victory   BPO 2538 142
Overture – Leonore 3   COA *PD 68181-2*
Piano Concertos –
complete
   Weissenberg       BPO Angel-EMI in preparation
      No. 1 Eschenbach
                    BPO 139 023
      No. 4 Gieseking  PO   *32 16 0371*  *33 C 1001* (10/6/51)
      No. 5 Gieseking  BPO *32 16 0029*  *33 CX 1010* (9/6/51)
         Weissenberg
                    BPO 37062      ASD 3043 (27/5/74)
Violin Concerto
   Ferras            BPO 139 021
Triple Concerto
   Richter, Rostropovich,
   Oistrakh          BPO 36727      ASD 2582 (17/9/69)

Overtures:
   Fidelio
   Leonore 1, 2, 3

                    Prometheus
                    King Stefan
                    Ruins of Athens
                    Egmont
                    Coriolan
                    Namensfeier
                    Consecration of the
                    House                BPO 2707 046

**BERG**
      Three Orchestral Pieces, Op. 6
      Three Pieces from the
      "Lyric Suite"           BPO 2530 487


**BERLIOZ**
      Damnation of Faust
          Dance of the Sylphs —
          Dance of the
          Will-o'-the-wisps    BPO 2530 244
      Hungarian March          PO   35426          SAX 2302 (18/1/58)
      The Trojans
          Royal Hunt and
          Storm                PO   35793          SAX 2294 (6/1/59)
      Symphonie Fantastique
                               PO   *35202*         *33 CX 1206* (21/7/54)
                               BPO 138 964
                               BPO 2530 597
      Roman Carnival
      Overture                 PO   35613          *33 CX 1548* (9/1/58)


**BIZET**
      Carmen — complete
          Price, Corelli, Freni, Merrill,
          Linval, Macaux, Benoit
          Besancon, Schooten, Demigny,
          VSOC, VBC, Pitz,
          Froschauer           VPO LDS 6164        (3)
      Suite No. 1              PO   35618          SAX 2289 (16/1/58)
                               BPO 2530 128
      Entr'acte Act 4.         PO   *35207*         *33 CX 1265* (23/7/54)
      L'Arlesienne Suites,
          1 & 2                PO   35618          SAX 2289 (15/1/58)
                               BPO 2530 128


**BOCCHERINI**
      Quintettino, La Musica
      Notturna di Madrid       BPO 2530 247

134

**BORODIN**
Prince Igor Polovtzian
Dances               PO   35925          *33 CX 1327* (8/11/54)
                     BPO 2530 200

**BRAHMS**
Symphonies
    No. 1            COA *PD 68175-80*
                     PO   *35001*        *33 CX 1053* (7/5/52)
                     VPO STS 15194       SDD 283 (3/59)
                     BPO 138 924
    No. 2            VPO *GQX 11441-5*
                     PO   *35218*        *33 CX 1355 (25/5/55)*
                     BPO 138 925

    No. 3 + Tragic
    Overture         VPO CS6249          SDD 284 (10/60, 10/61)
    No. 3            BPO 138 926
    No. 4            PO   *35298*        *33 CX 1361* (26/5/55)
                     BPO 138 927
Tragic Overture      BPO SEOM 18         (10/70)
Hungarian Dances
    1,3,5,6,17,18,19,
    20               BPO 138 080
Variations on a Theme
of Haydn             PO   *35299*        *33 CX 1349* (18/5/55)
                     BPO 138 926

Piano Concerto No. 2
    Richter-Haaser   BPO 35796           SAX 2328 (31/12/58)
    Anda             BPO 139 034
Violin Concerto
    Ferras           BPO 138 930
    Kremer           BPO ASD 3261        (7/3/76)
Ein Deutsches Requiem
    Schwarzkopf, Hotter,
    VS               VPO *SL 157*        *LX 1055-64*
    Janowitz, Waechter,
    VS               BPO 2707 018

**BRITTEN**
Variations on a theme of Frank Bridge
                     PO   *35142*        *33 CX 1159* (23/11/53)

**BRUCKNER**
Symphonies
    No. 4            BPO 2530 674
    No. 4 & 7        BPO 3779 C          SLS 811 (16/10/70)
    No. 8            BPO 3576 B          ST 772-3 (25/5/57)
    No. 8            BPO 2707 085

```
        No. 9            BPO 139 011
        Te Deum          BPO 2530 704
```

**CHABRIER**
Espana + Joyeuse Marche
```
                         PO                33 CX 1335 (9/7/55)
                         PO    35926       SAX 2404 (23/9/60)
```

**CHERUBINI**
```
    Anacreon Overture    BSOO PD 67514
```

**CHOPIN**
Les Sylphides (arr. Douglas)
```
                         BPO 136 257
```

**CILÉA**
Adriana Lecouvreur
```
    Act II – Intermezzo BPO 139 031
```

**CORELLI**
Concerto Grosso in G Minor
```
    Opus 6 No. 8         BPO 2530 070
```

**DEBUSSY**
```
    La Mer               PO    35081      33 CX 1099 (22/7/53)
                         BPO 138 923
```
Prélude à l'après-midi
```
    d'un faune           BPO 138 923
```

**DELIBES**
```
    Coppélia – Ballet Suite BPO 136 257
```

**DONIZETTI**
Lucia di Lammermoor
Callas, di Stefano, Panerai,
Zampieri, Zaccaria, Carlin,
Villa. Recorded "live",
Berlin Sept. 29,
```
    1955                 RIASO LE 101
```

**DVORAK**
```
    Scherzo Capriccioso  BPO 2530 244
    Symphonies
    No. 8                VPO CS6443        SXL 6169 (10/61)
    No. 9                BPO PD 67519-24
                         BPO 35615         SAX 2275 (7/1/58)
                         BPO 138 922
    Cello Concerto
        Rostropovich     BPO 139 044
```

136

Slavonic Dances
1,3,7,10,16        BPO 138 080

**FRANCK**
Symphony in D minor  OdP 36729        ASD 2552 (29/11/69)
Symphonic Variations
  Gieseking          PO  *ML 4536*
  Weissenberg        BPO 36905        ASD 2872 (27/9/72)

**GIORDANO**
Fedora — Intermezzo
Act II               BPO 139 031

**GOUNOD**
Faust — Ballet Music  PO   35607        SAX 2274 (18/1/58)
                      BPO 2530 199

**GRANADOS**
Goyescas — Intermezzo PO  *35207*      *33 CX 1265* (22/7/54)
                      PO  35793        SAX 2294 (5/1/59)

**GRIEG**
Peer Gynt
  Suite No. 1        VPO CS 6420      SXL 2308 (9/61)
       No. 1 & 2     BPO 2530 243
Piano Concerto in A Minor
  Gieseking          PO  *ML 4885*    *33 C 1003* (6/6/51)
Sigurd Jorsalfar —
Incidental Music     BPO 2530 243

**HANDEL**
Concerto Grossi Opus. 6
  Nos. 1, 8, 11      BPO 139 042
       2, 4, 6       BPO 139 035
       3, 7, 9       BPO 139 036
       5, 10, 12     BPO 139 012
Water Music — Suite
  (arr. Harty)       PO   *35004*     *33 CX 1033* (31/7/52)
                     BPO 35948        SAX 2389 (31/12/59)

**HAYDN**
Symphonies
  No. 83            BPO 36868        ASD 2817 (23/8/71)
  No. 101           BPO 36868        ASD 2817 (23/8/71)
  No. 103           VPO CS 6369      SDD 312 (1963)
  No. 104           VPO STS 15106    SDD 362 (3/59)
  No. 104           BPO ASD 3203     (12/75)

137

The Creation
Janowitz, Ludwig, Wunderlich,
Krenn, Fischer-Dieskau, Berry, VS,
Schmid, Froschauer, Nebois,
Borwitzky          BPO 2707 044

The Seasons
Janowitz, Hollweg,
Berry, DOC, Hagen-
Groll              BPO 3792 C          SLS 969 (11/72)

## HINDEMITH
Mathis der Maler-Symphony
                   BPO 35949          SAX 2432 (29/11/57)

## HOLST
The Planets         VPO CS 6244        SXL 2305 (9/61)

## HONEGGER
Symphonies Nos. 2 & 3 BPO 2530 068

## HUMPERDINCK
Hansel and Gretel — complete
Schwarzkopf, Gruemmer,
Metternick, Ilosvay,
Schurhoff, Felbermayer,
Choruses of Loughton
and Bancrofts       PO  *3506 B*        *33 CX 1096-7* (16/7/53)

## KODALY
Hary Janos — Intermezzo
                    PO  *35207*         *33 CX 1266* (24/7/54)

## LEHAR
Merry Widow
Harwood, Kollo,
Kélémen, Hollweg,
Stratas, Grobe, Krenn,
Renar, Gessendorf,
Borris, Ott, Pritchett,
Reinoso, Grosshans,
Krukowski, Vant,
Roehrl, DOC, Hagen-
Groll              BPO 2707 070
Highlights from above
                   BPO 2530 729

## LEIMER
Piano Concerto in C Minor

Piano Concerto for Left Hand
Leimer              PO    SME 91 793    (11/11/54, 12/11/54)

**LEONCAVALLO**
Pagliacci — complete
    Carlyle, Bergonzi, Taddei,
    Panerai, Benelli, Morresi,
    Ricciardi, LSMC,
    Genaglio            LSMO 2709 020
Highlights from above   LSMO 136 281
Intermezzo              PO    *35207*        *33 CX 1265* (22/7/54)
                        PO    35793          SAX 2294 (3/1/59)
                        BPO 139 031

**LISZT**
Les Préludes            PO    35613          (17/1/58)
                        BPO 139 037
Mazeppa                 BPO 138 692
Mephisto Waltz          BPO 2530 244
Hungarian Rhapsody
No. 2                   PO    35614          SAX 2302 (10/1/58)
Nos. 2, 4, 5            BPO 138 692
Nos. 4, 5              BPO 2530 698
Hungarian Fantasia
    Cherkassky          BPO 138 692
Tasso                  BPO 2530 698

**LOCATELLI**
Concerto Grossi in F Minor
Opus 1. No. 8          BPO 2530 070

**MAHLER**
Symphony No. 5         BPO 2707 081
Kindertotenlieder
    Ludwig             BPO 2707 081
Das Lied von der Erde
    Ludwig, Kollo      BPO 2707 082
Fuenf Rueckert Lieder
    Ludwig             BPO 2707 082

**MANFREDINI**
Concerto Grosso in C
Op. 3 No. 2            BPO 2530 070

**MASCAGNI**
Cavalleria Rusticana — complete
    Cossotto, Martino,
    Bergonzi, Guelfi,

139

```
          Allegri, LSMC,
          Benaglio          LSMO 2709 020
          Highlights        LSMO 136 281
          Intermezzo
            Heiller         VPO LVX 100
            Brain           PO   35207        33 CX 1265 (22/7/54)
            Meyer           BPO 139 031
          L'Amico Fritz —
          Intermezzo        PO   35793        SAX 2294 (3/1/59)
                            BPO 139 031
```

## MASSENET
```
          Thais — Meditation   PO   35207     33 CX 1265 (23/7/54)
                               BPO 139 031
```

## MENDELSSOHN
```
          Hebrides Overture    BPO 35950      SAX 2439 (9/60)
          Symphonies — Complete
          (No. 2 Mathis, Rebmann, Hollweg, DOC)
                               BPO 2720 068(4)
          No. 3 + Hebrides
          Overture             BPO 2530 126
          No. 4 and 5          BPO 2530 426
```

## MOZART, LEOPOLD
```
          Toy Symphony         PO   35638     SAX 2375 (28/4/57)
```

## MOZART, WOLFGANG AMADEUS
```
          Adagio and Fugue in
          C Minor              VPO ML 4370    LX 1076
                               BPO 2530 066

          Ave verum corpus
            VS                 PO   35948     SAX 2389 (28/7/55)
          Concertos
            Clarinet K.622
            Vlach              VPO GQX 11484-7 (7/12/49)
            Walton             PO   35323     33 CX 1361 (10/7/55)
            Horn (four)
            Brain              PO   35092     33 CX 1140 (23/11/53)
            Seifert            BPO 139 038
            Piano No. 21 K467
            Lipatti            LFO 35931      33 CX 1064 (23/8/50)
            Piano No. 23 K488
            Gieseking          PO   ML 4536   33 C 1012 (9/6/51)
            Piano No. 24 K491
            Gieseking          PO   35501     33 CX 1526 (26/8/53)
            Concertos for Winds
            Flute No. 1 — Blau
```

140

Flute and Harp –
Galway, Hemlis
Oboe – Koch
Clarinet – Leister
Bassoon – Piesk
+ Sinfonia Concertante K297B
Steins, Staehr, Braun,
Hauptmann         BPO 3783 C        SLS 817 (24/8/71)
Coronation Mass      BPO 2530 704
Così Fan Tutte
   Schwarzkopf, Merriman,
   Otto, Simoneau,
   Panerai, Bruscantini,
   PC             PO   *3522 C*    *33 CX 1262-4* (21/7/54)
Divertimentos: K136,
           137, 138,
                 BPO 139 033
          K247,
          251,   BPO 139 013
          K287,  PO  *35562*    *33 CX 1511* (28/5/55)
                 BPO 139 004
          K334  BPO 139 008
German Dances       BPO 35948      SAX 2389 (11/60)
Magic Flute – complete
   Seefried, Lipp, Dermota,
   Kunz, Weber, Loose,
   Jurinac, London, Rieger,
   Schuerhoff, Majkut,
   Proglhoff, Klein,
   Steinmassl, Doerpinghans,
   Stueckl, VS      VPO *SL 115* (3)   *33 CX 1013-5* (11/50)
   – Overture      BSOO *PD 67465*
Marriage of Figaro –
complete
   Schwarzkopf, Seefried,
   Jurinac, Kunz, London,
   Hoengen, Majkut, Rus,
   Feldon, Schwaiger,
   Czeska, Felbermayer,
   VSOC         VPO *SL 114* (3)   *33 CX 1007-9* (9/50)
   – Excerpts from
 above recording   VPO *35326*
   – Overture      VPO *LX 1008*
Masonic Funeral Music VPO *LX 1155*
Requiem
   Lipp, Roessel-Majdan,
   Dermota, Berry, VS BPO 138 767

141

Tomowa-Sinton,
Baltsa Krenn, van
Dam, VS, Hagen-
Groll          BPO 2530 704
Serenades:
No. 6 Serenata Notturna

           BPO 139 033
No. 13, Eine Kleine
Nachtmusik        VPO *ML 4370*       *LX 1293*
                  PO    *35098*        *33 CX 1178* (18/11/53)
                  BPO 35948       SAX 2389 (31/12/59)
                  BPO 139 004
Sinfonia Concertante, K.297 B
   Sutcliffe, Walton,
   Brain, James       PO    *35098*        *33 CX 1178* (18/11/53)
Symphonies
No. 29 K201         BPO 35739       SAX 2356 (1/3/60)
                  BPO 139 002
No. 33 K319         VPO *ML 4370*       *LX 1006-8*
                  BPO 139 002
No. 35 K385     EIARSO *DL 9513*     *PD 67986-8*
                  PO    *35562*        *33 CX 1511* (29/5/55)
                  BPO 36770       ASD 3016 (25/9/70)
No. 36 K425         BPO 36770       ASD 2918 (25/9/70)
No. 38 K504         PO    35739        SAX 2356 (17/9/58)
                  BPO 36771       ASD 2918 (25/9/70)
No. 39 K543         VPO *RL 3068*        *LX 1375-7*
                  PO    *35323*        *33 CX 1361* (10/7/55)
                  PO    35739
                  BPO 36771       ASD 3016 (25/9/70)
No. 40 K550     EIARSO *PD 67983-5*
                  VPO STS 15106    SDD 361 (3/59)
                  BPO 36772       ASD 2732 (25/9/70)
No. 41 K551     EIARSO *PD 67993-6*
                  VPO CS 6369     SDD 361 (1962)
                  BPO 36772       ASD 2732 (25/9/70)
No. 35 to 41, +
rehearsal record    BPO SLS 809      (4) (10/70)


## MUSSORGSKY
   Boris Godonov — complete
     Vishnevskaya, Ghiaurov,
     Spiess, Frese, Karolidis,
     Lilowa, Kiakov, Paunov,
     Radev, Markov, Heppe,
     Prelcec, Maljakovic,
     Dobrianowa, Cvejic,

142

Kélémen, Talvela,
Maslennikov, VBC,
SRC, VSOC,
Balatsch             VPO OSA 1439        SET 514-7 (11/70)
Khovantchina
    Entr'acte Act 4.       PO    *35207*       *33 CX 1327* (23/7/54)
                        PO    35793        SAX 2294 (5/1/59)
                        BPO 139 031
    Dance of the Persian
    Slaves              PO    *35207*       *33 CX 1327* (8/11/54)
                        PO    35925        SAX 2421 (23/9/60)
    Pictures at an Exhibition
    (orch. Ravel)       PO    35430        SAX 2261 (18/6/56)
                        BPO 139010

## NICOLAI
    Merry Wives of Windsor —
    Overture           BPO 35950        SAX 2439 (11/60)

## OFFENBACH
    Gaité Parisienne       PO    35607        SAX 2274 (18/1/58)
                        BPO 2530 199
    Orpheus in the Underworld —
    Overture           PO             *33 CX 1335* (8/7/55)
                        PO    35926        SAX 2404 (23/9/60)
    Tales of Hoffman —
    Barcarolle         PO    35207        SAX 2294 (6/1/59)

## ORFF
    De temporum fine comoedia
        Lorand, Marsh, Griffel,
        Anderson, Killebrew, Loevaas,
        Tomowa-Sintow, Angervo,
        Loulis, Goisen, Helm,
        Wegmann, Anheisser, Frese,
        Patzalt, Jokel, Diakow,
        Carmeli, Ludwig, Schreier,
        Greindl, Boysen, CRC,
        Schernus, RIASK, Gronostay,
        TK, Schmidt-Gaden
            CRSO 2530 432

## PACHELBEL
    Kanon and Gigue in D Major
       Meyer            BPO 2530 247

## PONCHIELLI
La Gioconda — Dance of the Hours

|  | PO *35327* | *33 CX 1327* (6/11/54) |
|---|---|---|
|  | PO 35925 | SAX 2421 (23/9/60) |
|  | BPO 2530 200 |  |

## PROKOFIEV
Peter and the Wolf

| Peter Ustinov | PO 35638 | SAX 2375 (28/4/57) |
|---|---|---|
| Symphony No. 5 | BPO 139 040 |  |

## PUCCINI
La Bohème — complete
Freni, Pavarotti,
Harwood, Panerai,
Ghiaurov, Maffeo,
Sénéchal, Pietsch,
DOC, Hagen-Groll     BPO OSA 1299     SET 565-6 (3/73)
Gianni Schicchi —
O mio babbino caro
Schwarzkopf     VPO *LV 7*
Madame Butterfly —
complete
Callas, Danieli, Gedda,
Villa, Borriello,
Ercolani, Carlin,
Clabassi, Campi,
LSMC, Mola     LSMO *3523 C*     *33 CX 1296-8* (6/8/55)
Madame Butterfly —
complete
Freni, Pavarotti,
Ludwig, Kerns,
Sénéchal, Stendoro,
Rintzler, Helm,
Schieder, Schary,
Frese, Hurdes, Heigl,
Muhlberger, VSOC,
Benaglio     VPO OSA 13110     SET 584-6 (8/74)
Manon Lescaut —

| Intermezzo | VPO *LVX 100* |  |
|---|---|---|
|  | PO *35207* |  |
|  | PO 35793 | SAX 2494 (3/1/59) |
|  | BPO 139 031 |  |

Tosca — complete
Price, di Stefano, Taddei,
Cava, Corena, de Palma,
Monreale, Weiss, Mariotti,
VSOC, Benaglio     VPO OSA 1294     5BB 123-4

144

Suor Angelica –
Intermezzo               BPO 139 031
Turandot – Tu che di
gel sei cinta
Schwarzkopf          VPO LB 85            (16/3/49)

## RACHMANINOFF
Concerto for Piano No. 2
Weissenberg          BPO 36905            ASD 2872 (27/9/72)

## RAVEL
Alborada del Gracioso  OdP 36839          ASD 2766 (29/6/71)
Bolero                 BPO 139 010
Daphnis and Chloë
Suite No. 2            BPO 138 923
Rhapsodie Espagnole    PO   35081         33 CX 1099 (17/7/53)
                       OdP 36839          ASD 2766 (29/6/71)
Le Tombeau de
Couperin               OdP 36839          ASD 2766 (29/6/71)
La Valse               OdP 36839          ASD 2766 (29/6/71)

## RESPIGHI
Ancient Airs and Dances –
Suite No. 3            BPO 2530 247
Pines of Rome          PO   35613         *33 CX 1548* (10/1/58)

## REZNICEK
Donna Diana –
Overture               VPO *LX 1402*       (8/12/47)

## RIMSKY-KORSAKOV
Schéhérezade           BPO 139 022

## ROSSINI
Overtures
La Gazza Ladra,
La Scala di Seta
Semiramide
Barber of Seville
Italian in Algiers
William Tell           PO   35890         SAX 2378 (30/3/60)
                       BPO 2530 144
Semiramide         EIARSO *PD 68154-5*
Sonatas for Strings,
Nos. 1,2,3 and 6       BPO 139 041
William Tell – Ballet
Music                  PO   35607         SAX 2274 (18/1/58)

**ROUSSEL**
Symphony No. 4      PO   *LX 1348-51*    (29/11/49)

**SCHMIDT**
Notre Dame — Intermezzo
                  PO   35793       SAX 2294 (6/1/59)
                  BPO 139 031

**SCHOENBERG**
Pelleas und Melisande, Op.5
                  BPO 2530 485
Verklaerte Nacht,
Op. 4             BPO 2530 486
Variations for Orchestra,
Op. 31           BPO 2530 486

**SCHUBERT**
Symphonies
No. 8             PO   *35299*      *33 CX 1349* (19/5/55)
                  BPO 139 001
                  BPO ASD 3203    (12/75)
No. 9             VPO *ML 4631*     *LX 1138-43* (20/9/46)
                  BPO 139 043

**SCHUMANN**
Concerto for Piano
   Lipatti          PO   *32 16 0141*    *33C 1001* (10/4/48)
   Gieseking       PO   35321
Symphonies — complete
+ Overture, Scherzo
and Finale        BPO 2720 046     (3)
No. 4             BPO     .       *33C 1056* (26/4/57)

**SHOSTAKOVICH**
Symphony No. 10      BPO 139 020

**SIBELIUS**
Concerto for Violin
   Ferras           BPO 138 961
Finlandia         PO   *35002*      *33 CX 1047* (31/7/52)
                  PO   35922       SAX 2392 (6/1/59)
                  BPO 138 961
Swan of Tuonela    BPO 138 974
Symphonies
No. 2             PO   35891       SAX 2379 (29/3/60)
No. 4             PO   *35082*      *33 CX 1125* (7/7/53)
                  BPO 138 974
No. 5             PO   *35002*      *33 CX 1047* (29/7/52)
                  PO   35922       SAX 2392 (23/9/60)
                  BPO 138 973
No. 6             PO   *35316*      *33 CX 1341* (5/7/55)

|                        | BPO 139 032      |                          |
| No. 7                  | PO   *35316*     | *33 CX 1341* (6/7/55)    |
|                        | BPO 139 032      |                          |
| Tapiola                | PO   *35082*     | *33 CX 1125* (15/7/53)   |
|                        | BPO 138 973      |                          |
| Valse Triste           | PO   35614       | SAX 2302 (17/1/58)       |
|                        | BPO 139 016      |                          |

## SMETANA
### Bartered Bride
| – excerpts             | BPO 2530 244     |                          |
| Ma Vlast – Moldau      | BPO *PD 67583-4* |                          |
|                        | BPO 35615        | SAX 2275 (20/5/58)       |
|                        | BPO 139 037      |                          |
| – Vysehrad             | BPO 139 037      |                          |

## STRAUSS, JOHANN, SR.
| Radetzky March         | PO   35926       | SAX 2404 (24/9/60)       |
|                        | BPO 139 014      |                          |

## STRAUSS, JOHANN, JR.
| Annen Polka            | VPO STS 15163    | SDD 259 (3/59)           |
|                        | BPO 139 014      |                          |
|                        | BPO ASD 3132     | (8/1/76)                 |
| Auf der Jagd Polka     | VPO STS 15163    | SDD 259 (3/59)           |
|                        | BPO 2530 027     |                          |
| Artists Life Waltz     | BPO *PD 67585*   |                          |
|                        | VPO *AL 28*      | *LX 1013* (30/10/46)     |
|                        | PO   *35342*     | *33 CX 1393* (27/5/55)   |
| Blue Danube Waltz      | VPO *LX 1118*    | (30/10/46)               |
|                        | PO   *35342*     | *33 CX 1393* (8/7/55)    |
|                        | BPO 139 014      |                          |
|                        | BPO ASD 3132     | (8/1/76)                 |
| Egyptian March         | BPO 2530 027     |                          |
| Emperor Waltz          | BPO *PD 67649*   |                          |
|                        | VPO *AL 28*      | *LX 1021* (30/10/46)     |
|                        | PO   *35342*     | *33 CX 1393* (8/7/55)    |
|                        | BPO 139 014      |                          |
|                        | BPO ASD 3132     | (8/1/76)                 |

Die Fledermaus –
complete
    Schwarzkopf, Streich,
    Gedda, Krebs, Kunz,
    Doench, Christ, Majkut,
    Boeheim, Martini,

| PC                     | PO   *3539 B*    | *33 CX 1309-10* (30/4/55) |

    Gueden, Koeth, Resnik,
    Zampieri, Berry, Waechter,
    Kunz, Kmentt, Klein,
    Schubert, Godknow,

Fasolt, von Mattoni,
VSOC                    VPO OSA 1249       SXL 6015-6
same as above with
the addition of a
Gala Sequence in Act
II featuring guest
appearances by
Tebaldi, Corena,
Nilsson, del Monaco,
Berganza, Sutherland,
Bjoerling, Price,
Simionato, Bastianini,
Welitsch                VPO OSA 1319       (3)
Overture                VPO STS 15163      SDD 259 (3/59)
                        BPO 139 014
                        BPO ASD 3132       (8/1/76)

The Gypsy Baron —
Overture                BPO *PD 67997*
                        VPO *LX 1009*      (30/10/46)
                        PO   *35342*       *33 CX 1393* (7/7/55)
                        VPO STS 15163      SDD 259 (3/59)
                        BPO 139 014
                        BPO ASD 3132       (8/1/76)
Perpetuum Mobile        VPO *LV 15*        (21/1/49)
                        BPO 139 014
Persian March           BPO 2530 027
Morning Papers Waltz    BPO 2530 027
Pizzicato Polka         PO   *35342*       *33 CX 1393* (9/7/55)
                        BPO 2530 027
Tales from the Vienna
Woods                   VPO *LVX 137*
                        VPO STS 15163      SDD 259 (3/59)
                        BPO 2530 027
Tritsch-Tratsch Polka   VPO *LB 128*       (28/10/49)
                        PO   35926         SAX 2404 (24/9/60)
                        BPO 139 014
                        BPO ASD 3132       (8/1/76)
Vienna Blood Waltz      VPO *LX 1321*      (29/11/49)
                        BPO 2530 027
Wine, Women and
Song                    VPO *LX 1402*      (29/11/49)

**STRAUSS, JOSEF**
Delirien Waltz          VPO *LX 1303*      (31/1/50)
                        PO   *35342*       *33 CX 1393* (6/7/55)
                        VPO STS 15163      SDD 259 (3/59)
                        BPO 139 014

| Sphaerenklaenge | VPO *LX 1250* | (28/2/50) |
| Transaktionen Waltz | VPO *LX 1257* | (29/11/49) |

## STRAUSS, RICHARD

Also Sprach
| Zarathustra | VPO STS 15083 | SDD 211 (4/59) |
| | BPO 2530 402 | |

Ariadne auf Naxos —
complete
    Neugebauer, Doench,
    Seefried, Schock,
    Under, Cuenod, Strauss,
    Kraus, Streich,
    Schwarzkopf, Prey,
    Ollendorff, Krebs,
    Otto, Hoffman,

| Felbermayer | PO   *3532 C* | *33 CX 1292-4* (7/7/54) |

Concerto for Oboe
| Koch | BPO 2530 439 | |

Concerto for Horn No. 1
| Hauptmann | BPO 2530 439 | |
| Don Juan | COA *DL 9529* | *PD 68127-9* |
| | PO   *CX 1001* | (3/12/51) |
| | VPO CS 6211 | SPA 219 (6/61) |
| | BPO 2530 349 | |

Don Quixote
| Fournier | BPO 139 009 | |
| Rostropovitch | BPO ASD 3118 | (8/1/75) |

Four Last Songs
| Janowitz | BPO 2530 368 | |

Ein Heldenleben
| Schwalbé | BPO 138 025 | |
| Schwalbé | BPO 37060 | ASD 3126 (28/5/74) |
| Metamorphosen | VPO *LX 1082-5* | (3/11/47) |
| | BPO 2530 066 | |

Der Rosenkavalier — complete
    Schwarzkopf, Edelmann,
    Ludwig, Kuen, Waechter,
    Randall, Welitsch, Meyer,
    Majkut, Bierbach, Unger,
    Proglhof, Friedrich,
    Gedda, Felbermayer,

| PC, | PO   3563 D | SAX 2269-72 (12/56) |
| Excerpts from | | |
| above | PO   35646 | |

Dance of the Seven Veils
| | COA *PD 68126* | |

|                          | VPO CS 6211      | SDD 211 (10/60)    |
|--------------------------|------------------|--------------------|
|                          | BPO 2530 349     |                    |
| Sinfonia Domestica       | BPO ASD 2955     | (25/6/73)          |
| Till Eulenspiegel        | PO  *CX 1001*    | (4/12/51)          |
|                          | VPO CS 6211      | SDD 211 (10/61)    |
|                          | BPO 2530 349     |                    |
| Tod und Verklaerung      | VPO CS 6211      | SDD 211 (10/60)    |
|                          | BPO 2530 368     |                    |

## STRAVINSKY

| Apollon Musagète         | BPO 2530 065     |
|--------------------------|------------------|
| Circus Polka             | BPO 2530 267     |
| Concerto for Strings in D | BPO 2530 267    |
| Le Sacre du Printemps    | BPO 138 920      |
| Symphony in C            | BPO 2530 267     |

## SUPPÉ
Overtures
    Light Cavalry
    Morning, Noon and
    Night in Vienna
    Pique Dame
    Beautiful Galathea
    Jolly Robbers

| Poet and Peasant         | BPO 2530 051     |                      |
|--------------------------|------------------|----------------------|
| Light Cavalry Overture   | PO   35926       | SAX 2404 (21/9/60)   |

## TCHAIKOVSKY

| Capriccio Italien        | BPO 139 028      |                      |
|--------------------------|------------------|----------------------|
| Concerto No. 1 for Piano |                  |                      |
|   Richter       | VSO 138 822      |                      |
|   Weissenberg   | OdP 36755        | ASD 2576 (2/70)      |
|   Berman        | BPO 2530 677     |                      |
| Concerto for Violin       |                  |                      |
|   Ferras        | BPO 139 028      |                      |
| Eugen Onegin — Waltz and Polonaise | BPO 2530 200 |               |
| 1812 Overture            | PO   35614       | SAX 2302 (6/2/59)    |
|   Don Cossack Choir | BPO 139 029 |                      |
| Marche Slav              | BPO 139 029      |                      |
| Nutcracker Suite         | PO  *35004*      | *33 CX 1033* (31/7/52) |
|                          | VPO CS 6420      | SXL 2308 (9/61)      |
|                          | BPO 139 030      |                      |
| Romeo and Juliet         | VPO *LX 1033-5*  | (29/10/46)           |
|                          | VPO CS 6209      | SPA 219 (1/61)       |
|                          | BPO              | 139 030              |

| | | |
|---|---|---|
| Serenade for Strings | BPO 139 030 | |
| Sleeping Beauty Suite | PO 35006 | 33 CX 1065 (24/11/52) |
| | PO 35740 | SAX 2306 (7/1/59) |
| | VPO CS 6452 | SXL 6187 (3/65) |
| | BPO 2530 195 | |
| Swan Lake Suite | PO 35006 | 33 CX 1065 (24/11/52) |
| | PO 35740 | SAX 2306 (7/1/59) |
| | VPO CS 6452 | SXL 2306 (3/65) |
| | BPO 2530 195 | |
| Symphonies: | | |
| No. 4 | PO 35099 | 33 CX 1139 (16/7/53) |
| | BPO 35885 | SAX 2357 (1/3/60) |
| | BPO 139017 | |
| | BPO 36884 | SLS 833 (21/9/71) |
| No. 5 | PO 35055 | 33 CX 1133 (8/8/53) |
| | BPO 139 018 | |
| | BPO 36885 | SLS 833 (21/9/71) |
| | BPO 2530 699 | |
| No. 6 | BPO PD 67499-504 | TC 9055 |
| | VPO ML 4299 | 33 CX 1026 (21/1/49) |
| | PO 33 CX 1377 | (18/6/56) |
| | BPO 138 921 | |
| | BPO 36886 | SLS 833 (21/9/71) |
| Variations on a Rococo Theme | | |
| Rostropovich | BPO 139 044 | |

**TORELLI**
Concerto Grosso

| | | |
|---|---|---|
| Op. 8 No. 6 | BPO 2530 070 | |

**VAUGHAN-WILLIAMS**
Fantasia on a Theme

| | | |
|---|---|---|
| by Thomas Tallis | PO 35142 | 33 CX 1159 (23/11/53) |

**VERDI**
Aida — complete
    Tebaldi, Simionato,
    Bergonzi, Macneil,
    van Mill, Corena,
    de Palma, Ratti,

| | | |
|---|---|---|
|     VS, Schmidt | VPO OSA 1313 | SXL 2167-9 (9/59) |
|     Ballet Music | PO 33 CX 1237 | (5/11/54) |
| | PO 35925 | SAX 2421 (21/9/60) |
| | BPO 2530 200 | |

Falstaff — complete
    Gobbi, Alva, Panerai,
    Spataro, Ercolani,
    Zaccaria, Schwarzkopf,

Moffo, Merriman,
Barbieri, PC     PO   *3552 C*       *SMS 1001* (24/7/56)
La Forza del Destino —
           BSSO *PD 67466*
   Overture         BPO 2563 555
Otello — complete
   del Monaco, Tebaldi,
   Protti, Satre, Romanato,
   Corena, Krause, Cesarini,
   Arbace, VSOC, VGKC,
   Benaglio        VPO OSA 1324     SET 209-211 (5/61)
   Vickers, Glossop,
   Bottion, van Dam,
   Sénéchal, Machi, Helm,
   Freni, Malagù, DOC,
   Hagen-Groll      BPO 3809 D       SLS 975 (5/73)
   Ballet Music     BPO 2530 200
   Overtures and
   Preludes — complete BPO 2707 090
Requiem
   Freni, Ludwig, Cossutta,
   Ghiaurov, VS,
   Froschauer      BPO 2707 065
La Traviata — Prelude
to Act III        PO    35793        SAX 2294 (3/1/59)
           BPO 139 031
Il Trovatore — complete
   Panerai, Callas, Barbieri,
   Villa, di Stefano,
   Zaccaria, Ercolani,
   Mauri, LSMC, Mola
         LSMO *3554 C*      *33 CX 1483-5* (9/8/56)

**VIVALDI**
   Concerti P28, 86, 143, 208, 246,
   Sinfonia P21      BPO 2530 094
   Four Seasons
     Schwalbé       BPO 2530 296

**WAGNER**
   Flying Dutchman —
   Overture        BPO 35950        SAX 2439 (19/9/60)
           BPO 37098        ASD 3160 (10/74)
   Die Goetterdaemmerung —
   complete
     Brilioth, Stewart,
     Kélémen, Moser,
     Ridderbusch,

Dernesch, Janowitz,
Ludwig, Chookasian,
Rebmann, Reynolds,
Ligendza, DOC, Hagen-

| | | |
|---|---|---|
| Groll | BPO 2716 001 | (6) |
| Lohengrin — complete | BPO EMI/ANGEL in preparation | |
| Prelude to Act I | BPO 35950 | SAX 2439 (19/9/60) |
| | BPO 37097 | ASD 3130 (10/74) |
| Prelude to Act III | VPO *LX 1360* | (3/1/50) |
| | BPO 37098 | ASD 3160 (10/74) |
| Bridal Chorus | | |
| VSOC | VPO *LX 1360* | (3/1/50) |

Die Meistersinger —
complete
  Edelmann, Schwarzkopf,
  Hopf, Kunz, Dalberg,
  Majkut, Berg, Pfanzl,
  Janko, Mikorey, Stolze,
  Tandler, Borst, van Mill,
  Unger, Malaniuk,
  Faulhaber, BFC, Pitz

| | | |
|---|---|---|
| | BFO *6030 E* | *33 CX 1021-5* (24/8/51) |

  Adam, Ridderbusch, Buechner,
  Lunow, Evans, Kélémen,
  Rotzsch, Bindszus,
  Hiestermann, Polster, Reeh,
  Vogel, Kollo, Schreier, Donath,
  Hesse, Moll, DSOC, LRC,

| | | |
|---|---|---|
| Neumann | DSO 3776 E | SLS 957 (4/12/70) |
| Act I — Prelude | BPO *PD 67532* | |
| | BPO 35482 | 33 CX 1496 (19/2/57) |
| | DSO SEOM 18 | (12/70) |
| | BPO 37098 | ASD 3160 (10/74) |
| Da zu dir der Heiland | | |
| Kam | VSOC *LX 1258* | (2/12/49) |
| Act III Wach auf | BSOO *PD 67527* | |
| | VSOC *LX 1258* | (2/12/49) |
| Parsifal — Preludes to | | |
| Acts I & III | BPO 37098 | ASD 3160 (10/74) |

Das Rheingold — complete
  Fischer-Dieskau, Kerns,
  Grobe, Stolze, Kélémen,
  Wohlfahrt, Talvela,
  Ridderbusch, Veasey,
  Mangelsdorff, Dominguez,
  Donath, Moser,

| | |
|---|---|
| Reynolds | BPO 2709 023 |

Excerpts as above    BPO 136 437
Der Ring des Nibelungen –
complete
   for cast details see
   Das Rheingold, Die
   Walkuere, Siegfried
   and Goetterdaemmerung
                BPO 2720 051    (19)
Siegfried – complete
   Thomas, Stolze, Stewart,
   Kélémen, Ridderbusch,
   Dominguez, Dernesch,
   Gayer    BPO 2713 003
   Excerpts as above    BPO 135 150
Tannhaeuser –
   Overture    BPO *35482*    *33 CX 1496* (8/1/57)
– Venusberg Music    PO    35925    *33 CX 1327* (5/11/54)
– Overture & Venusberg
   Music (Paris version)
   DOC    BPO 37097    ASD 3130 (19/10/74)
– Grand March and
   Entry of the Guests    VPO LX 1347    (12/12/49)
Tristan und Isolde –
complete
   Vickers, Dernesch, Ludwig,
   Berry, Weikl, Schreier,
   Vantin, DOC, Hagen-
   Groll    BPO 3777 E    SLS 963 (10/1/72)
   Preludes to Acts
   I & III    BPO SEOM 18    (1/72)
   Prelude and
   Liebestod    BPO *35482*    *33 CX 1496* (8/1/57)
                BPO 37097    ASD 3130 (10/74)
Die Walkuere – complete
   Vickers, Talvela, Stewart,
   Janowitz, Crespin, Veasey,
   Rebmann, Ordassy, Steger,
   Brockhaus, Mastilovic,
   Ericson, Ahlin,
   Jenckel    BPO 2713 002    (5)
   Excerpts from above BPO 135150
Act III
   Rysanek, S. Bjoerling, Friedland,
   Varnay, Lausch, Wild,
   Siewert, Thomamuller,
   Toepper, H. Ludwig,
   BFC    BFO *33 CX 1005-6* (15/8/51)

**WALDTEUFEL**
    Skater's Waltz        PO  35926          SAX 2404 (23/9/60)

**WEBER**
    Overtures
        Der Freischuetz
        Oberon
        Euryanthe
        Abu Hassan
        Peter Schmoll
        Ruler of the
        Spirits           BPO 2530 315
        Der Freischuetz  COA *PD 68354-5*
                    BPO 35950       SAX 2439 (9/60)
    Invitation to the
    Dance           PO  35614      SAX 2303 (18/1/58)
                    BPO 2530 244

**WEBERN**
    Passacaglia for Orchestra, Op. 1
    Five Movements, Op. 5
    Six Pieces for Orchestra, Op. 6
    Symphony, Op. 21   BPO 2530 488

**WEINBERGER**
    Schwanda the Bagpipe
    Player – Polka    PO  35926       SAX 2404 (23/9/60)

**WOLF-FERRARI**
    Jewels of the Madonna –
    Intermezzo
    Act III         BPO 139031

**MISCELLANEOUS COLLECTIONS**
    Christmas Songs
        Stille Nacht, Heilige Nacht
        Hark! The Herald Angels Sing –
        Mendelssohn
        We Three Kings of Orient are
        Angels We Have Heard on High
        O Tannenbaum
        God Rest ye Merry Gentlemen
        It Came Upon a Midnight Clear
        Vom Himmel Hoch – Bach
        Sweet li'l Jesus
        Ave Maria – Schubert
        O Holy Night
        Ave Maria – Gounod

Halleluja — Mozart
Price, VBC, VS    VPO OS 25280        SXL 2294 (6/61)
Prussian and Austrian Marches
Yorck March
Togau March
You, My Austria
Under the Flag of Caprice
The Great Elector's Cavalry
The Entry into Paris
Under the Double Eagle
The Emperor's Marksmen
Florentine March
Finnish Cavalry March
Koniggratz March
Children of the Regiment
Vienna forever
Fanfare: The Crusaders
St. Petersburg March
Fehrbelliner Cavalry March
Pappenheim March
March of the German Masters
Vindobona March
Hohenfriedberg March
Archduke Albrecht March
Tirolean Woodcutter Lads
The Glory of Prussia
Coburg March
March: Carinthian Songs
The Bosnians are Coming
Fridericus Rex
Old Comrades
March from the Gypsy Baron
Nibelungen March
                    BPO 2721 077        (2)


The European Anthem
*The European Anthem* (arrangement for
full orchestra by Karajan of the theme
from the 4th Movement of Beethoven's
Ninth Symphony), together with the
national anthem of the 17 member states
of the Council of Europe
                    BPO 2530 250


156

# Index

(of persons mentioned in the text)